INDIA IN
LUXURY

Published in 2009 by Prakash Books India Pvt. Ltd.
1, Ansari Road, Daryaganj, New Delhi-110 002, India. Tel.: +91-11-23247062.
Email: sales@prakashbooks.com. Website: www.prakashbooks.com,

Designed by: www.ysdesignstudio.com

ISBN: 978-81-7234-289-0

Printed & bound in India at EIH Ltd.

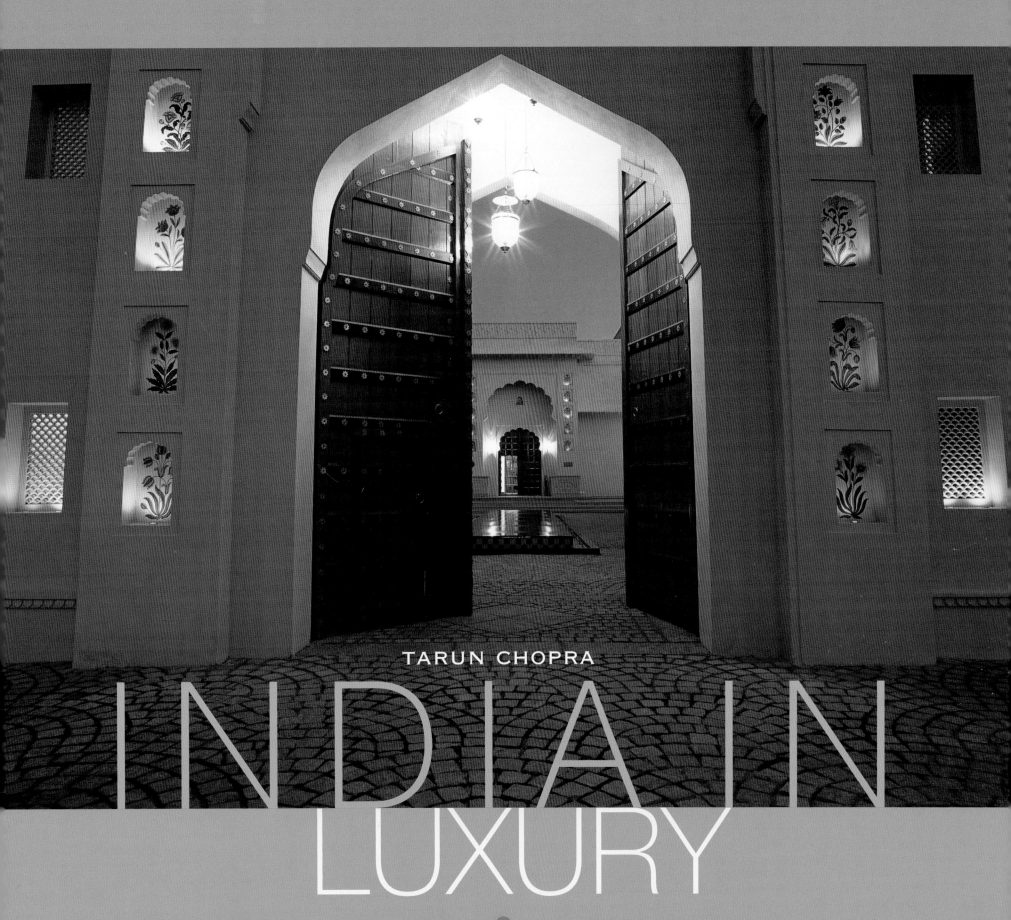

TARUN CHOPRA

INDIA IN
LUXURY

PRAKASH BOOKS

CONTENT

JAIPUR

BELOW: VIEWS OF THE PRIVATE RESIDENCE OF THE JAIPUR CITY PALACE; THE WALLS OF THE FORMAL SITTING ROOM ARE ADORNED WITH 250-YEAR-OLD GOLD PAINTINGS AND THE FURNITURE CONSISTS OF SOLID SILVER CHAIRS. THE TRANSLUCENT DINING TABLE WAS ONE OF THE TWO EVER MADE BY THE FRENCH ARTIST RENE LALIQUE FOR THE ROYAL FAMILY.
OPPOSITE PAGE: THE MAGNIFICENT ENTRANCE HALL OF THE UMAID BHAVAN PALACE IN JODHPUR THAT WAS THE LAST PALACE TO BE BUILT IN THE COUNTRY IN THE YEAR 1943. IT IS ENTIRELY MADE OF BUFF-COLOURED SANDSTONE; THE SWIMMING POOL OF THE PALACE IS IN THE BASEMENT, DIRECTLY BELOW THE FLOOR OF THIS MARVELLOUS HALL.

Dule Raja, the handsome warrior-prince of the Kachhwaha clan of the Rajputs, founded the ancient capital Amber in AD 1128. For centuries, this warrior caste protected the frontiers of the rugged kingdom. However, it was not until six centuries later when the twenty-second Maharaja, Raja Jai Singh, ascended the throne and moved the capital to the present city of Jaipur. The old capital at Amber could not accommodate the growing number of people. Besides, the town suffered severe water shortage.

Raja Jai Singh planned the city, as we know it today. With the help of his chief architect Vidyadhar from Bengal, who belonged to the Shaspati order of Hindu Priest Architects, he divided the city into nine blocks. These were further divided into 107 sub-blocks (known in Shilpa-Shastra as 'Pithapada') in what was perhaps the first attempt at urban planning in India.

The Maharaja personally supervised the plans of this new city, which he named after himself. The principles of the Shilpa-Shastra, an ancient architectural treatise, were incorporated in the plans and the result was a beautifully symmetrical city that was both practical and aesthetic.

Jai Singh's fascination for science, mathematics and astronomy led him to build massive open-air observatories not only in the capital city but

also in Delhi, Mathura, Ujjain and Varanasi. Besides telling the time, these complicated astronomical instruments calculated the height and position of heavenly bodies, read the altitude and distances in the sky and informed both the time and the sun's path in the heaven. A thirty-metre high sun dial indicated the hour when the sun's shadow moved every four metres, thus gauging the time of the day. Another achievement was the Jayaprakash Yantra instrument that measured planetary and astral positions in the universe.

Jaipur is also known as the Pink City because in 1876, the entire city was painted pink, symbolic of hospitality, to welcome the Prince of Wales. Maharaja Pratap Singh built Jaipur's signature building, the Hawa Mahal or Palace of Winds, in 1799. Centrally located in the town, it has a pink sandstone façade, is five-storey high but only one room deep. Hawa Mahal was the discreet vantage point from where the ladies in purdah, peering through the honey-combed windows, could get a glimpse of the activities outside the palace walls.

The City Palace is the official residence of the Maharajas of Jaipur. It was partly converted into a museum in 1959 and houses many royal treasures.

Crystal chandeliers, pashmina rugs, illustrated manuscripts, and jewelled weapons are beautifully displayed in various sections of the palace.

The other major attraction is the Diwan-e-Khas in which are exhibited huge silver jars, each weighing 350 kg – the largest in the world. There is an interesting story about them that speaks of the religious sentiments of nineteenth and early twentieth century Hindu maharajas. When the Maharaja was invited to the coronation of King Edward VII, a luxury liner was chartered and outfitted to suit his royal tastes. As a measure against stepping on impure, alien land on his arrival, sand from Jaipur was put inside his shoes and the silver jars were filled with the holy waters of the Ganges so that the Maharaja could purify himself at all times. Also, silver and gold offerings were made to the sea to ward off evil spirits. The silver jars, therefore, symbolized the king's compromise that enabled him to travel overseas and yet remain pure.

The present Maharaja resides with his family in their private apartments in Chandra Mahal.

Rambagh Palace, the other royal palace outside the city wall, was built as the hunting lodge of Maharaja Ram Singh in the eighteenth century.

It was later converted into a royal guest house. Raja Madho Singh II, who had then ascended the throne, instructed Sir Jacob Swinton, a British resident architect, to refurbish it. Maharaja Sawai Man Singh II - 'Jai' – decided to make it his residence in the 1930s. He lived here with his three wives. His third wife, Maharani Gayatri Devi, the beautiful princess of Coochbehar, was just thirteen years old when they fell in love. They were married in 1940. After Sawai Man Singh II died in England in 1970 during a polo game, the Maharani moved to the Lily Pool behind the palace, where she still lives. Today, Rambagh Palace is a luxury hotel and boasts of exotic suites, a fabulous dining hall and alfresco marble verandas.

The Amber Palace, 11 km north of Jaipur, comes into view around the last bend in the winding road. Built by Mughal artisans during the reign of Man Singh I in the sixteenth century, the palace is set amid the charming Aravalli Hills. It boasts of paintings and marble panels set in relief by artists from the Mughal court. What draws the visitor's attention is the art of mirror inlay-work in wet plaster, which reflects a thousand stars against the ceiling even when a single flame is lit in the room.

A leisure elephant ride up to the fort offers a panoramic view of

the city and its majestic walls with guard towers. It is an unforgettable experience for any visitor. Within the palace is the Kali Mata Temple. The image of the goddess, the manifestation of divine energy, was brought from Jessor in Bengal and installed here by Maharaja Man Singh I in 1604. The temple is made of white marble, which is exquisitely carved by local artisans. The entrance door is made of silver and depicts the Goddess Kali in her many forms of feminine energy. Above the door is a statue of Lord Ganesha carved out of a single piece of coral.

Jaipur is well known for its colourful bazaars, which their founder, Jai Singh, had planned. He wanted the city to be recognized for its elaborate artistry and fine craftsmanship. His wish is alive today in the dazzling array of precious stone jewellery, brassware, carpets, miniature paintings and antiques that can be found in various parts of the city.

The life inside the gates is bustling with commercial frenzy that manages to engulf everyone. Jewels studded with precious stones, hand-knotted carpets, miniature paintings, old textiles, fabricated antiques and hand block-printed cotton textiles top the purchase list of every visitor to this enchanting city.

The Oberoi Rajvilas is set in 32 acres of lush green paradise with pavilions, reflecting pools and fountains. A 350-year-old temple stands in the centre of the garden around which the resort was built.

14

17

19

ABOVE: THE ENTRANCE COURTYARD OF **THE OBEROI RAJVILAS** HAS A GEOMETRIC-SHAPED REFLECTING POOL WITH OCTAGONAL RAJASTHANI 'CHATTRI' OR CUPOLA IN THE CENTRE; TWO STATUES ON TOP OF COLOSSAL SANDSTONE PILLARS GREET VISITORS TO THIS ROYAL ABODE.

ABOVE: ENTRANCE TO THE MAIN BUILDING FROM THE GUEST ROOM AREA IS SURROUNDED BY A MOAT FILLED WITH WATER LILIES; TWO MONOLITHIC SANDSTONE SENTINELS STAND GUARD.

BELOW: TWO MONOLITHIC SANDSTONE ELEPHANTS FILL THE SWIMMING POOL OF THE OBEROI RAJVILAS; THE COLUMN IN THE BACKGROUND TRANSFORMS INTO A FLAMING TORCH AT NIGHT. OPPOSITE PAGE: PLUNGE POOL IN ONE OF THE PRIVATE VILLAS OF THE RESORT IS SHADED WITH FRANGIPANI TREE.

ABOVE: LAVISHLY DECORATED LIVING ROOM OF THE 17TH-CENTURY NAILA FORT. OPPOSITE PAGE: THE BAR AREA IN THE OBEROI RAJVILAS IS REMINISCENT OF THE RAJ ERA, COMPLETE WITH TEAK WOOD PANELLING, RICH LEATHER CHAIRS AND HAND-KNOTTED CARPET — A PERFECT SETTING FOR A LEISURELY DRINK.

TREATMENT ROOMS OF THE SPA IN THE OBEROI RAJVILAS ARE TRULY DIVINE; MUGHAL-STYLE FLOWER FRESCOES, PAINTED WITH DYES MADE FROM CRUSHED, SEMI-PRECIOUS STONES AND 24-CARAT GOLD LEAF, DECORATE THE WALLS. **BELOW:** A ROSE PETAL BATH INVITES YOU TO A REJUVENATING EXPERIENCE.

34

ABOVE: LIVING ROOM OF THE ROYAL VILLA IS AN AMALGAMATION OF TRADITIONAL RAJASTHANI DECORATION WITH MODERN COMFORTS; HAND-KNOTTED PERSIAN RUG, MADE FROM VEGETABLE-DYED YARN, COVERS THE SANDSTONE FLOOR. OPPOSITE PAGE: THE LIVING ROOM OF THE NAILA FORT BECKONS THE LUXURIOUS ERA OF THE RAJ IN A TRADITIONAL RAJASTHANI FORT; THE LIVING ROOM IS ADORNED WITH CHOICEST CRYSTAL, BRONZE AND SILVER OBJECTS.

ABOVE: THE BEDROOM OF THE ROYAL VILLA IS DECORATED WITH A HAND-WOVEN 'DURRIE' OR RUG AND WOODEN HANDICRAFTS FROM THE THAR DESERT; THE BONE-INLAID TEAK CUPBOARD AT THE FAR END HOUSES THE MINI BAR. OPPOSITE PAGE, LEFT: HAND-PICKED ART OBJECTS SUCH AS THE MARBLE NANDI AND MUGHAL FLOWER ART-WORK DECORATE THE GUEST ROOM IN THE OBEROI RAJVILAS. OPPOSITE PAGE, RIGHT: WOODEN BUDDHA STATUE GILDED WITH GOLD ENHANCES THE BEAUTY OF THE NAILA FORT.

41

DECORATION OF **THE OBEROI RAJVILAS** RIVALS ANY MUGHAL PALACE; REAL AND PAINTED FLOWERS ARE USED TO BEAUTIFY THE RESORT. **OPPOSITE PAGE:** A STUNNING MUGHAL 'TREE OF LIFE' PAINTING IS EXECUTED ON LAPIS LAZULI; COLOURED BACKGROUND ENHANCES THE RECEPTION AREA OF THE SPA.

BELOW: THE ETHNIC CHIC TENTED ACCOMMODATION OF THE OBEROI RAJVILAS IS THE EPITOME OF INDULGENCE. OPPOSITE PAGE: THE LIVING ROOM OF THE TENTED VILLA IS DECORATED WITH HAND- WOVEN 'DURRIES'; SHEER GAUZE CURTAINS, ANTIQUE WOODEN HORSE AND THE DRAPED CANOPY OF THE TENT IS PRINTED BY HAND USING WOODEN BLOCKS AND NATURAL PIGMENTS.

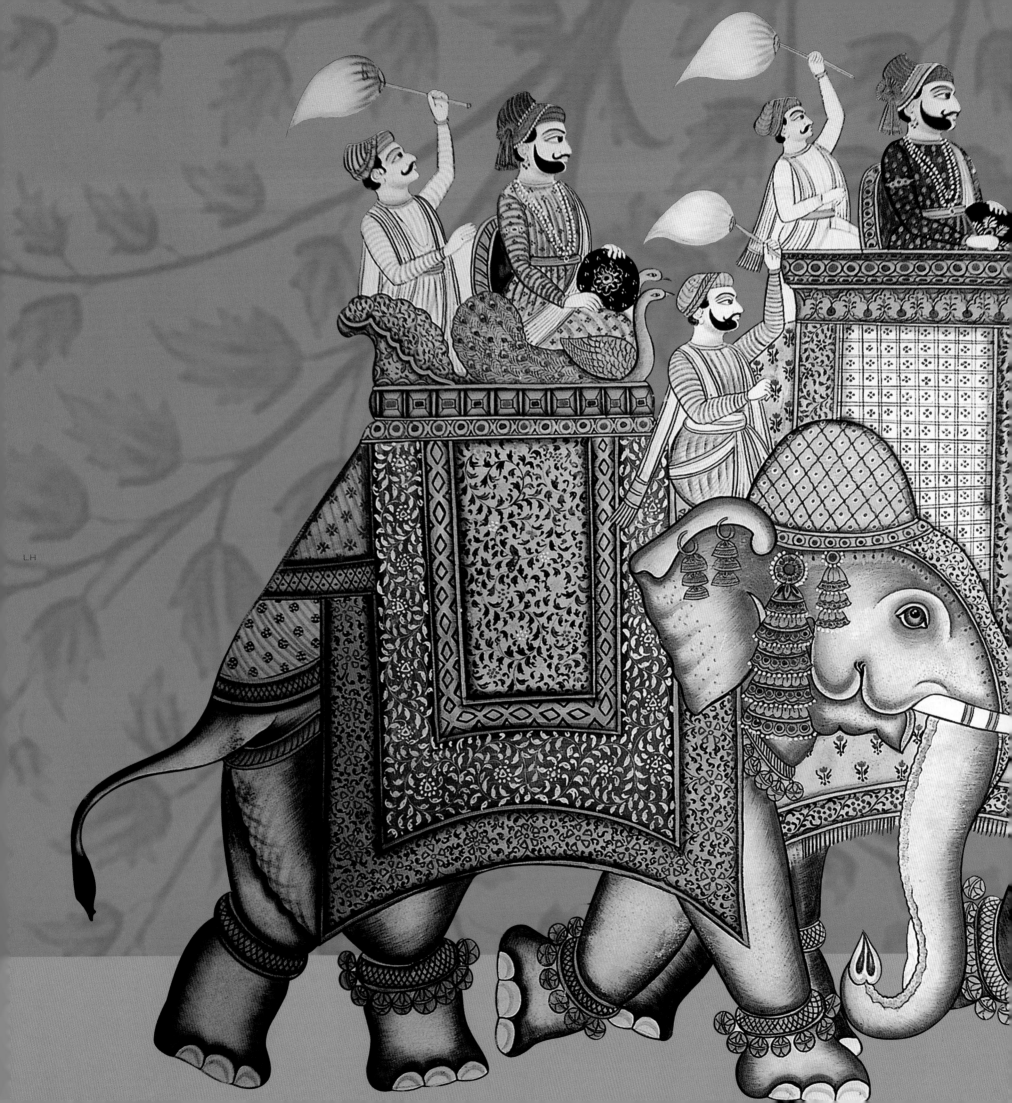

UDAIPUR

Udaipur is considered as the most romantic city of India. It is the city of magical lakes and gardens, with majestic palaces either floating on or built on the fringes of these picturesque lakes. The city is renowned for its old town that can be approached from the palace gates and is best explored on foot. Shops selling traditional puppets, silver jewellery and colourful textiles crowd either side of the lanes. There are also antique shops that sell some eclectic mix of artefacts. Apart from the shopping experience, it is a delight to watch traditional craftsmen carrying on with their centuries old trade. In this labyrinth of streets, one can easily come across elephants or cows mingling with modern day traffic. Towering shikhars of Hindu temples dot the skyline as seen from the lake.

Lake Palace and Jag Mandir are famous landmarks of the city. These were conceived as pleasure islands for the Maharanas in the 18th century. The former is executed in white marble and delicately decorated with bright coloured crystal. The latter is now transformed into a party island available for celebrations in exotic locales.

Some two hundred years later, the Lake Palace was converted into a luxury hotel. Among its first guests was Queen Elizabeth II. It is a delight to

spend a couple of nights in this enchanting island where one is ferried across by boat to this unique hotel. The ride is breathtaking, especially when one sees the palaces on the edge of the lake reflected in the water. The City Palace, the residence of Maharana of Udaipur, rests at the other end of Lake Pichola. The older part of the palace has been converted into a museum, which contains the largest collection of Mewari paintings, while another section is now the Shiv Niwas Palace, a luxury hotel. The new part of the palace is known as Fateh Prakash Palace and houses some of the finest crystal collection of the nineteenth century.

The topography of Udaipur provides a refreshing change because of its numerous lakes, as compared to other arid regions of Rajasthan.

Historically, Udaipur was the seat of the Maharanas of Mewar who belonged to the Sisodia clan of Rajputs. The title 'Maharana' was given to them for they were known never to have surrendered in any battle. Nor did they accept the dominance of any foreign rule, either of the Muslims or of the British. As a mark of respect, they were the chiefs of thirty-six clans of Rajputs.

Their Udaipur kingdom has a rich history of resistance to the Muslims.

IN THE ENVIRONS OF UDAIPUR ARE SOME OF THE MOST BEAUTIFUL JAIN TEMPLES OF INDIA. **BOTTOM, LEFT:** AN INTRICATELY CARVED WALL PANEL OF LORD PARSHAVANATH IN RANAKPUR TEMPLE. **BOTTOM, RIGHT:** THE ENTRANCE PORCH OF THE TEMPLE HAS THIS BEAUTIFUL CARVING CHISELLED FROM A SINGLE PIECE OF WHITE MARBLE, WHERE A SOLE FACE BELONGS TO FIVE DIFFERENT BODIES. **OPPOSITE PAGE:** THE 11TH-CENTURY DILWARA TEMPLE IN MOUNT ABU IN THE VICINITY OF UDAIPUR BOASTS OF AN ORNAMENTALLY DETAILED CEILING, PILLARS AND PANELS. THIS CAPTIVATING TEMPLE SEEMS TO HAVE BEEN ACCOMPLISHED WITH THE BLESSING OF THE DIVINE.

49

The surrounding areas of Haldighati, Chittor and Kumbhalgarh bear testimony to the fierce battles fought between the Rajputs and the Mughals. The legends of warrior kings, Rana Sangha and Rana Pratap, are still sung by the people of the area. The Sisodias of Mewar are also proud of the fact that unlike other ruling families of Rajasthan, they never gave their daughters in marriage to the Mughal harem.

The long and turbulent history of the Rajputs also includes defiance of the British. As late as 1911, when the Delhi Durbar was held to honour George V, the only empty chair belonged to Maharana Fateh Singh ji of Udaipur, whose displeasure with British rule was well known. The chair, which signified the Rajput sense of pride, is still on display at the City Palace. The Maharanas of Mewar can trace their family to Bapa Rawal of 728, who received the state of Mewar in trust from his mentor, Guru Harit Rashi at Eklingji. It is the oldest ruling family of India or perhaps of the world. Bapa Rawal established his capital in Chittor, which once was the largest fortified city in the world. The repeated siege of Chittor made the Maharanas move to the more ideally situated and naturally defended city in the sixteenth century.

The surrounding Aravalli hills have beautiful forts, palaces and temples,

THE CITY PALACE COMPLEX OF UDAIPUR IS A SERIES OF PALACES BUILT BY MANY GENERATIONS ON THE HILLY OUTCROP OF LAKE PICHOLA. THE ROOMS ARE AS COLOURFUL AS THE LIFESTYLES OF THE ERSTWHILE RULERS. IN RAJASTHAN, VIVID COLOURS WERE USED IN LIBERAL DOSES TO COMPENSATE THE STARK ARID SURROUNDINGS. **BELOW:** THE ROOM HAS MUGHAL FLOWER PANELS PAINTED AT THE BOTTOM WHILE RELIGIOUS MINIATURE PAINTINGS DECORATE THE WALL; AN ANTIQUE STEAM-OPERATED VENTILATION DEVICE STANDS IN THE CORNER. **OPPOSITE PAGE:** THE ROOMS IN THE PALACE WERE DECORATED WITH INLAID GLASS MOSAIC AND MINIATURE PAINTINGS. FAUX FLOOR COVERINGS AND DOOR PAINTINGS WERE USED AS DECORATIVE ELEMENTS.

which are worth exploring. The Eklingji Temple is the 'kul devta' of the Maharanas of Mewar; close to the temple are the temples of Nagdha. Devigarh, a beautiful fort that has been lovingly restored into a luxury hotel, is also located close by.

About four hours drive to the east is the Dilwara Temple located in Rajasthan's only hill station, Mt. Abu. At Dilwara, there are five Svetambar Jain temples, dating from twelve to the fourteenth century. Of these, Vimal Vashi and Luna Vashi temples are the most beautiful.

It is easy to believe local folklore, which explains how the artisans

chiselled out incredible carvings in marble. The dust, which came out of the carving, was weighed in equal amounts with gold and for broken pieces, silver was used for payment. Hence, it is no wonder that the artisans gave us one of the most beautiful temples unmatched in any part of the world. The sculptor adorned the temples with delicately carved human, animal and floral motifs, which make the hard marble, appear as fine as porcelain.

Two hours' drive through the scenic Aravalli Mountains is Ranakpur, one of the finest examples of temple architecture of medieval India constructed in the early fifteenth century. The inspiration came for it from the dream of

the minister in which he saw a celestial vehicle for the gods. The architect, Deepa, translated the dream into reality.

The inner sanctum is unique in India as it houses four statues of Adinath, the first of the twenty-four Jain prophets. Two thousand five hundred sculptors worked on the site and the temple was completed after 63 years. The temple is three-storey high and has four entrance doors. Each storey of the temple is adorned with a four-faced statue of the prophet. The domes and the torans are profusely decorated with fine marble sculptures. There are said to be 1444 columns, of which no two are alike. In respect to the almighty lord, one column has been left crooked symbolizing that perfection can only rest with the divine.

Udaivilas is probably one of the most opulent and luxurious resorts in the world. It is constructed on a site that was once used to give young Mewar princes their first lessons in hunting wild animals. A beautiful hunting lodge with fabulous miniatures painted on its walls still stands in Udai Vilas. Some thirty odd acres are divided into suites, spa, restaurants and guest rooms, many of which have their own meandering pools. The melon-shaped domes add drama to its idyllic setting.

52

THE OBEROI UDAIVILAS HAS BEEN CREATED AS A 21ST CENTURY PALACE RESORT AND NO STONE HAS BEEN LEFT UNTURNED IN THIS QUEST. **BELOW:** THE GEOMETRIC PATTERN ON THE MARBLE FLOOR OF THE PATIO OUTSIDE THE DINING ROOM IS EXECUTED WITH THE INLAY OF BLACK MARBLE STRIPES. A SOLITARY TREE IN THE CENTER ACCENTUATES THE EFFECT. **OPPOSITE PAGE:** THE DRAMATIC MARBLE PETALS OF GIANT LILY FLOWER SEEM TO FLOAT MAGICALLY ON THE SURFACE OF THE PRISTINE BLUE POOL OF THE ENTRANCE COURTYARD.

THE OBEROI UDAIVILAS IS FULL OF PLEASANT SURPRISES. WATER FOUNTAINS AND REFLECTING POOL LOOK MAGICAL AT DUSK WHEN THE LIGHTS OF THE RESORT COME ON. **OPPOSITE PAGE, LEFT:** A GIANT ANTIQUE CRYSTAL CHANDELIER DECORATES THE SPA WHICH IS SPREAD OVER TWO FLOORS. THE DOME IS A BEAUTIFULLY PAINTED SKY WITH PUFFY CLOUDS AND BIRDS FLYING ACROSS. **OPPOSITE PAGE, RIGHT:** THE TREATMENT ROOMS IN THE SPA ARE SENSITIVELY DECORATED AND CATER TO AN ARRAY OF MASSAGES. THEY ARE THOUGHTFULLY LOCATED OVER LOOKING THE POOL AND THE WATERBODIES.

BELOW: PRISTINE BLUE TILED POOL SURROUNDS THE KOHINOOR SUITE; THE TERRACE AROUND IT PROVIDES A COMMANDING VIEW OF THE RESORT, LAKE PICHOLA AND THE ROYAL PALACES BEYOND. **OPPOSITE PAGE:** LOCAL ART HAS BEEN GIVEN FULL IMPORTANCE IN THE DETAILED DECORATIONS OF **THE OBEROI UDAIVILAS**; THE ETHNIC MIRROR INLAY ART OF UDAIPUR HAS BEEN BEAUTIFULLY INCORPORATED IN THE PUBLIC AREAS.

The Oberoi Udaivilas is built incorporating the natural contours of the hill that subsequently provided various levels of the building. Here in the foreground is the dining area while in the background are guest rooms with a plunge pool running lengthwise in the front; the lush green landscape is punctuated with bright floral vegetation. **Previous pages:** Udaipur literally means 'the city of sunrise'. The pool area of Udaivilas is a perfect place to watch the drama of the rising sun unfold over the series of palaces reflecting into the placid waters of the lake. **Below & Opposite page:** the dining room extends into the marble patio which is a popular place to have breakfast or dine under the stars, watching the performances of local musicians and dancers.

62

BELOW: THE BEDROOMS ARE DRAPED IN CHOICEST SILKS AND LINEN; HAND BLOCK PRINTED THROWS WITH MUGHAL FLOWER MOTIFS ADORN THE BED. OPPOSITE PAGE: DRAMA UNFOLDS AT EACH STEP YOU TAKE IN THE RESORT; THE RECEPTION AREA HAS VAULTED DOMES SUPPORTED BY CUSPED ARCHES; THE RIBBED DESIGN INSIDE THE DOME IS COATED WITH 24 CARAT GOLD LEAF; MOSAIC PATTERNS ON THE FLOOR ARE ACCOMPLISHED IN THE CHOICEST BLACK AND WHITE MARBLE.

67

68

ABOVE: THE FOUNTAIN IN THE ENTRANCE HALL OF THE OBEROI UDAIVILAS WELCOMES VISITORS INTO ITS LUXURIOUS FOLDS. OPPOSITE PAGE: THE BANISTER OF THE CIRCULAR STAIRCASE IS CLAD WITH ANTIQUE PLASTERING TECHNIQUE WHILE EVERY SQUARE INCH OF ITS WALL IS DECORATED BY A GIANT MURAL OF LOCAL FLORA AND FAUNA EXECUTED BY LOCAL ARTISTS. THE PATTERN ON THE FLOOR IS INLAID WITH BLACK GRANITE WHILE THE CENTRE TABLE IS INLAID WITH MOTHER OF PEARL.

ABOVE: THE BAR IS LUXURIOUSLY APPOINTED WITH CHENILLE COVERED SOFAS, BURL WOOD AND LEATHER ARMCHAIRS THAT ARE INTIMATELY ARRANGED AROUND LOW TABLES THAT SIT ON EXQUISITE OCTAGONAL PERSIAN RUGS. BRASS CANDELABRAS AND LIFE SIZED PIGEONS EXECUTED IN SILVER ARE OTHER DECORATIVE ITEMS THAT BRING IN THE TRADITIONAL CHARM.

ABOVE: CANDLE ROOM LEADS TO THE GUEST ROOMS OF THE OBEROI UDAIVILAS. IN THE EVENING, THE LIGHTS FROM THE CANDLES SHIMMER LIKE STARS IN THE INTRICATE MIRROR INLAID DOME LOCATED DIRECTLY ABOVE THE TABLE. LOVESEATS ADORN THE CUSPED ARCH OPENINGS.

ABOVE: PASTEL SHADES OF THE WALLS AND SOFT HUES OF SILK FURNISHINGS DOMINATE THE SUITE IN THE OBEROI UDAIVILAS. THE ITALIAN MARBLE FLOORING IS COVERED WITH AN EXQUISITE ANTIQUE RUG BOASTING OF MUGHAL FLOWERS. THE OPEN DOOR ON THE RIGHT LEADS INTO THE MASTER BEDROOM. OPPOSITE PAGE : THE GUEST BEDROOMS OF THE OBEROI UDAIVILAS ARE DECORATED IN UNDERSTATED STYLE , WHICH IS BLENDED WITH THE LOCAL ELEMENTS. THE COTTON PATCHWORK BEDCOVER AND THE BLOCK PRINTED QUILTED THROW ARE LOCALLY SOURCED. BRIGHT COLOURED SILK AND COTTON CUSHIONS ADD VIBRANCY TO THE ROOM. THE CUSPED ARCH ABOVE THE HEAD BOARD AND PEACOCK MOTIF CORNER STONES AROUND THE ROOF ARE INPUTS FROM THE LOCAL ARTISANS.

76

AGRA

Agra rose to prominence when the great Mughal emperor, Akbar, made it his capital in 1556. He chose the site for his new capital on the banks of river Jamuna. The twenty-metre high outer walls of the Agra Fort, two-and-a-half kilometres in circumference, and the river were an almost impregnable line of defence. Thus, this formidable seat of power became the capital city of the Mughal Empire. The fort was a township in itself. The members of the royal family and their entourage were housed in palaces and other buildings along the river, including the Jasmine Tower, where Emperor Shah Jahan (the builder of Taj Mahal) was imprisoned before his death. The Diwan-e-Aam (Hall of Public Audience) used to be decorated with carpets and curtains woven with

gold and silver threads while the royal suites had walls inlaid with precious stones and jewels. The royal family enjoyed entertainment, and animal fights in particular below its ramparts were a source of much amusement.

Near the Agra Fort stands one of the wonders of the world – the Taj Mahal. It is a mausoleum built during the reign of Shah Jahan for his wife, Mumtaz Mahal, who died in 1630.

Taj Mahal, 'a dream in marble', was built to honour Mumtaz's dying wish for a memorial to their love. It took twenty-two years to complete the edifice and twenty thousand workers helped to create this masterpiece. Its perfection and beauty would not have been possible without the deft planning of

Ustad Ahmad Lahori and Isa Khan, master architects of the Mughal court, who designed the symmetry and proportion and every detail of the fine calligraphic and pietra dura ornamentation. The entire complex includes the forecourt and lofty entrance, a Mughal garden with canals, a central tank with a series of fountains, and the tomb proper, flanked by a mosque to its west and a guest house to the east. The graves rest in an underground crypt and are encased in marble, delicately decorated with semi-precious stones. The emperor had planned a similar tomb for himself, in black marble, on the opposite bank of the River Jamuna. In his later years, his son imprisoned him. Finally, he was buried beside his beloved.

Itmad-ud-Daulah is another exquisite marble tomb in Agra. Its beauty is unfairly eclipsed by the fame and size of the Taj. The tomb is lavishly decorated with pietra dura floral and geometric design. This gives the building a delicate appearance when viewed from a distance. The tomb is dedicated to Mirza Ghiyas Beg, a Persian noble and his wife. Their beautiful daughter, Mehrunissa, eventually became the empress Nur Jahan. This helped Mirza to climb the ranks of the noblemen and he was honoured with the title of 'Itmad-ud-Daulah,' or 'the pillar of the state.'

The tomb was built in 1628. It was the first bold expression in white marble situated in a charbagh (four gardens) and completely decorated with

pietra dura. It is often described as the 'baby Taj', and looks like a jewel box from the entrance gate.

About 50 km south of Agra is the ghost town of Fatehpur Sikri. Built entirely of locally quarried red sandstone, it is a splendid accomplishment of design and architecture of medieval India. Its dramatic location on top of the ridge, in barren landscape, adds to its imperial status.

The reason for the imperial city to be built so close to the already existing Mughal capital, Agra, is credited to Sheikh Salim Chisti, a Sufi saint who predicted the birth of Akbar's male heir.

The building of Fatehpur Sikri was a creative expression of extraordinary scale in medieval India. It was built within a span of fourteen years as the new capital of the Mughal Empire. Some 8000 workers worked on the site creating a beautiful lake on the edge of the city. The cost of construction is estimated at two million rupees. One rupee coin, in those days, was made up of 96% pure silver and weighed 178 grams.

After a short stay of fourteen years, Akbar marched out with his army in 1585 to control the Afghan rebellion. He positioned himself at Lahore, closer to the north-west border. After taking care of the problem, Akbar returned to Agra and never looked back at Fatehpur Sikri. The city was thus abandoned; many parts of the city have somehow survived the ravages of time.

The city was built on a grid pattern with the buildings aligning from east to west in north-south axis. The buildings at Fatehpur Sikri can be divided into three types: public congregational buildings like the Jama Masjid and Diwan-i-Aam; semi-official areas such as Diwan-i-Khas and Anup Talao; and private enclosures such as Jodha Bai's Palace and Begum Mariyam's Palace. The local stone-cutters worked with the artisans from Rajasthan and Gujarat. The latter translated Gujarati woodwork designs into that of red sandstone. Some other buildings were copies of Mughal camp tents. The architecture of the city is spectacular, especially its vaulted ceilings, which are supported by stone slabs acting as ribs. The majority of the structures use post and beam design with duchhati (two floors) and tibra (three-arch) elements. Some of the architectural wonders of Fatehpur Sikri are the Buland Darwaza, the giant gateway to Jama Masjid. The unique Diwan-i-Khas or Ekstambha Prasada, popularly known as the Hall of Private Audience, was probably a replica of a bird roost of Gujarat.

The city is vividly described in the accounts of Western travellers such as Catalan Padre Antonio Monserrat and English traveller, Ralph Finch. Court historians Abu'l Fazl and Badauni have also left detailed accounts of the everyday life of the palace and its citizens. Originally, the main entrance of the city was from the lakeside. There were two stone elephants flanking this

ceremonial entrance and it was thus called Hathi Pol. Heeran Minar (deer tower), in front of the Hathi Pol, was probably a lighthouse (akash deep) to guide travellers to the main entrance of the city.

The religious tolerance of Akbar gave a boost to creative activities in the new capital. Thousands of artisans worked in the court to produce illustrated manuscripts, calligraphy, gold seals, carpets and tapestry. Religious debates were encouraged; the Ibadat Khana was used for this purpose. 'Jizyah' or tax on non-Muslims was removed. 'Din-i-Ilahi' was declared the state religion that showed tolerance for, and gave equal respect to, all religions. These reforms struck a chord with the Hindu majority who were ruled by the Muslim minority. The Indianization of the Mughal dynasty was initiated.

The opulence of the Mughal court is not hard to imagine. It is said that at sunset, Anup Talao, the water tank in front of the emperor's palace, was filled with perfumed water. Floating lamps would illuminate the tank and the court musician, Tansen, seated in the central platform of the tank, would weave magic with his evening ragas. The only other sound filling the evening air would emanate from the ghungroo (ankle bells) of the nauch girls. It would appear as if the stars had descended from the heaven into Anup Talao.

The exquisite white marble tomb of the Sufi saint, Sheikh Salim Chisti, is located in the north of the courtyard of the mosque, Jama Masjid.

BELOW: THE TEA LOUNGE IN **THE OBEROI AMARVILAS** IS DECORATED WITH MUGHAL FLOWERS PAINTED ON 24-CARAT GOLD LEAF. A SIMILAR TREATMENT IS GIVEN TO THE ROOF FROM WHERE A CRYSTAL CHANDELIER GLOWS. **OPPOSITE PAGE:** THE GUEST ROOMS ARE ADORNED WITH HAND-KNOTTED RUGS IN AN ORNATE PAISLEY DESIGN; THE HEADBOARD, EMBELLISHED WITH CHAIN STITCH EMBROIDERY AND APPLIQUÉ THROWS IN MUGHAL MOTIFS, ENHANCE THE COMFORT OF THE BED. ETCHING OF ARCHITECTURAL DETAILS OF THE MUGHAL MONUMENTS ARE HUNG ON THE WALL AND THE WRITING DESK HAS INLAID BONE DESIGN.

ABOVE: TWO LEVELS OF THE HOTEL ARE ACCENTUATED WITH MILKY WHITE MARBLE STAIRCASE ALONG THE SIDES; A LIFE SIZE PANTHER AT THE BOTTOM IS CARVED OUT FROM A SINGLE BLOCK OF MARBLE. OPPOSITE PAGE: THE EXOTIC GRANDEUR OF THE OBEROI AMARVILAS IS APPARENT ON STEPPING INTO THE LOBBY; SANDSTONE AND WHITE MARBLE BLOCKS MAKE AN ATTRACTIVE PATTERN ON THE FLOOR; A COLOSSAL CHANDELIER LIGHTS UP THE ENTIRE AREA.

96

ABOVE: THE FLOOR OF THE SUITE IN THE OBEROI AMARVILAS IS COVERED WITH VEGETABLE DYE RUG DISPLAYING MUGHAL MOTIFS; INDIAN AND EUROPEAN FURNITURE ACCENTUATE ITS GRANDEUR. OPPOSITE PAGE: A PAINTED MARBLE ARTEFACT.

ABOVE, LEFT: PLUSH ARMCHAIR WITH HAND-EMBROIDERED CUSHION IN TURQUOISE SILK STANDS AGAINST THE SILK BROCADE WALL HANGING, EXECUTED IN GOLD AND SILVER THREADS. ABOVE, RIGHT AND OPPOSITE PAGE: TEAK WOOD PANEL BAR HAS A STRIKING CLOTH PAINTING REPRODUCED FROM A 17TH-CENTURY MINIATURE PAINTING OF TAJ MAHAL, SHOWING THE CROSS-SECTION OF THE MONUMENT AND THE SQUARE GARDEN PLAN IN FRONT. 24-CARAT GOLD LEAF IS PAINTED ON THE ROOF FROM WHERE A BEAUTIFUL CRYSTAL CHANDELIER HANGS; TABLES INLAID IN MARBLE ADD ELEGANCE TO THE BAR AREA.

102

Ranthambhore National Park is picturesquely located between the folds of Aravalli Range as it embraces the Vindhyan Plateau. Many years ago, it was the hunting ground of the Jaipur maharaja. Jogi Mahal is a beautiful hunting lodge dating back to the Medieval era. Located on the edge of the forest lake, it has been the venue for hunting expedition where the important dignitaries were taken for tiger shoot.

In 1981, the 330 sq km park gained the status of a national park. The topography of the park is as diverse as its vegetation. The general terrain is rocky that changes dramatically from flat-topped Vindhya Hills to conical peaks of the Aravalli Hills. There are vast stretches of grassland that acquire a beautiful golden hue after the monsoon rains. Ranthambhore National Park is the last remaining stretch of sizeable jungle left in Rajasthan.

The dry deciduous forest is abundant with dhok, peepal, mango and acacia trees. Ancient banyan with giant aerial roots seem to stand eternally in the forest. Two rivers, Banas and Chambal, bound the park on its northern and southern sides.

In the park is found a rich habitat of flora and fauna. There are about 272 species of birds, 12 types of reptiles and 30 different types of mammals. The

most famous, attractive and at times easily spotted is the tiger. According to the last census, some new cubs were born to the resident tigers, which reflect favourably of the forest conservation efforts. The tiger population is now 26. Due to the dry shrubby forest, it is easy to spot tigers in the park. But then again you can't take it for granted because tigers are nocturnal and unpredictable but once spotted they remain in sight for a considerable length of time as they are not shy of the crowd. Ranthambhore National Park is therefore considered a photographer's and filmmaker's paradise.

The fame of Ranthambhore is not only restricted to the tiger, the king of the jungle, but also can be attributed to the picturesque 11th century fort located at the top of a rocky outcrop in the middle of the forest. The fort is massive and covers an area of approximately 7 km in circumference. It is one of the oldest forts in the country and is said to have been built in AD 944 by a Chauhan warrior. Due to its location and structure, it is considered to have been one of the most difficult forts to capture. Any attempt to attack was repulsed by the local warriors. Finally, Muslim armies were able to conquer it by laying siege around the fort for years and thus cutting the food supplies. The most successful ruler of this fort is known to have been Rao Hammir in

BELOW: SAMBHAR DEER GRAZES IN THE SWAMPY LAKE OF RANTHAMBHORE. THIS DEER IS THE FAVOURITE FOOD OF THE TIGER. OPPOSITE PAGE: THE 11TH-CENTURY RANTHAMBHORE FORT STANDS MAJESTICALLY ON A STEEP HILL IN THE CENTRE OF THE PARK. THE FORT ITSELF IS WORTH THE JOURNEY TO RANTHAMBHORE. PREVIOUS PAGE, LEFT: CHEETAL OR SPOTTED DEER GRAZE UPON THE DRY SHRUB FOREST OF RANTHAMBHORE. THIS GRACEFUL DEER IS SEEN IN GREAT NUMBERS IN THE PARK. PREVIOUS PAGE, RIGHT: THE ROYAL BENGAL TIGER IS THE MAJOR ATTRACTION OF RANTHAMBHORE FOREST RESERVE. SEMI-ARID SHRUBLAND OF THE FOREST MAKES SPOTTING OF THE TIGER EASY.

110

the 11th century. His giant statue lies in pieces at the entrance gate.

According to a legend, over a thousand women once committed mass suicide as they would rather have killed themselves than fall prey to the armies of Muslim invaders.

In 1528, the fort was taken over by the Mughals. The great emperor Akbar is said to have stayed at the fort between 1558 and 1559.

The fort was finally gifted by the Mughals in the late 17th century to the Maharaja of Jaipur, who ruled his kingdom not far away from the magnificent fort at Amer. The fort then remained with the royal family of Jaipur till

Independence. This period turned out to be a boon for forest conservation as hunting was extremely well controlled and the wilderness was allowed to flourish.

On climbing up the ramparts of the fort, the first thing that strikes one, are the fabulous vistas of the jungles that surround the fort in all directions. The ruins found in the interior of the fort are stunning too. The acoustics of Hammir court are fabulous as even a whisper could be heard across the hall. There is also the mysterious Ganga or the perennial stream that can be seen at the bottom of the dark cave. There are numerous mosques and temples

112

located in the fort; the most famous among them is dedicated to Lord Ganesha, the elephant-headed god, son of Lord Shiva and Parvati. It is said that Lord Ganesha got married in the Ranthambhore Fort. At the time of weddings, each Hindu family sends Lord Ganesha an invite. Thus, everyday the temple priest reads out thousands of invitation cards to the god of good luck.

In the jungle itself, there are beautiful medieval structures that were palaces and pleasure gardens of erstwhile rulers. These ruins of bygone era are scattered all over the jungle, which give Ranthambhore National Park a unique blend of nature, history and wildlife – a combination that no national park can boast of.

The park has three rain-fed lakes, namely, Padam Talab, Malik Talab and Rajbagh where most of the animals converge during the day. These are also the habitat of crocodiles, wild boar, spotted deer called Chital and the tiger's favourite deer, Sambhar. If luck favours, one could be rewarded with the sighting of an Indian sloth bear and the ever-elusive leopard.

Three hours by car from Jaipur or a short train ride brings you to Sawai Madhopur town where Ranthambhore is located. Minutes' drive from there

It is often said that the history of India lies in the history of Delhi. New Delhi, the capital of India, has always occupied a strategic position in the country's history. It is from here that many Hindu and Islamic dynasties have ruled, leaving their imprint in the form of relics, which allow us to recapture bygone times. Delhi's history goes back to the days of the Mahabharata (3000-1500 BC) when the Pandavas lived on the banks of the River Yamuna. Their kingdom, near Indraprastha, has been identified as Delhi. Indraprastha later became Dhillika, the first of the seven medieval cities of Delhi. Its significant location, about 1,000 kilometres from the Khyber Pass (the entrance point for most foreign invaders), increased its importance as a vital strategic position in the defense of the country.

Qila Rai Pithora, the first known city of Prithviraj Chauhan III, was captured by Mohammed Ghori. Qutub-ud-Din Aibak, Ghori's slave general, declared himself as the Sultan of Delhi after his master's death in AD 1192. As these foreigners made the newly conquered lands their home, they gradually began to incorporate Indian ways in their lifestyle, thereby evolving a whole new culture. These influences are most evident in Indo-Islamic architecture, which reflects in the cultural synthesis that has taken place in Delhi over the centuries. An example of this unique style is found in the Quwat-ul-Islam mosque, where Islamic arches and calligraphy are beautifully

blended with floral designs. At places, the columns of the mosque are made of the plundered Hindu and Jain temples that existed on the site.

The Khalji Sultanate, which came to power in AD 1290 after toppling the previous Sultans, raised the second Delhi township of Siri, north-east of the Qila Rai Pithora. The Tughlaqs, who ruled after the Khaljis, built the third city of Tughlaqabad to the extreme south of Delhi, followed by the cities of Jahanpanah and Kotla Firoz Shah on the banks of the River Yamuna. When the Mughals replaced the Lodhi Dynasty in the early sixteenth century, its founder Babur concentrated on developing Agra and made it his capital. But his son, Humayun, constructed a new capital on the banks of the River Yamuna around the ancient capital and named it Din Panah. He also built a citadel, the Purana Qila. Shah Jahan, successor to Jahangir, built Shahjahanabad along the river as a well-planned, seventh township of Delhi. It remained the Mughal capital until AD 1857, despite the decline of the Mughal Empire in AD 1707.

In 1857, when the British Crown took over the control of India from the East India Company, the Viceroy and the government were at Calcutta, the commercial capital, owing to its easy accessibility to tea gardens and coal fields. However, in 1911, the decision was made to establish a new capital at Delhi, which was more centrally located. Plans were made to build a new city

to befit the 'Jewel in the British Crown'. The area along the ridge, south of Shahjahanabad, was chosen as the site for the imperial capital. It was built on a regal scale and was completed by January 1931. Though the city has grown enormously after the country's Independence in 1947, it is this area that boasts of the best landmarks bequeathed by the British.

Lutyens and Baker designed much of the red sandstone architecture along the stretch between India Gate and Rashtrapati Bhawan, with the adjoining administrative buildings of North Block and South Block that house important ministries. The circular Parliament House and the shopping arcade, Connaught Place was also designed by the duo.

The imposing twentieth-century British architecture blends beautifully with the Mughal monuments of the city. The architects were sensitive enough to follow the Mughal tradition of using buff and red coloured sandstone.

The Rock Edict of the Buddhist emperor Ashoka (273-236 BC) in South Delhi, one of the best pre-Islamic relics, bears the inscription of the great emperor's appeal to follow the path of peace and righteousness. A similar call is expressed in the writings on two pillars, one that is located in the ruins of Kotla Firoz Shah, whilst the other stands in close proximity to the renowned University of Delhi.

Perhaps the most famous among the Islamic relics is the Qutub Minar.

Begun in AD 1199 by Sultan Qutub-ub-Din Aibak as a minaret, calling the faithful to prayer, it served as a victory memorial as well. Until recently, it was open to general public to climb the grand minaret but was later closed as the height of the tower became unsafe for public. In 1311, Ala-ud-Din Khalji added the Alai Darwaza, which allows entry to the southern end of the Qutub Minar enclosure. The elaborate tomb of Iltutmish, which stands within the same compound, is a classic example of early Islamic architecture.

Further south lies the abandoned township of Tughlaqabad, one of the seven cities of Delhi, which was developed with an emphasis on town planning and defense. A citadel and a reservoir still remain stark reminders of a once glorious era. Well laid-out gardens and beautiful mausoleums are among the more enduring achievements of Islamic rule in Delhi. The area north of Tughlaqabad has many tombstones, some of which date back to the thirteenth century. The most well known among them is the tomb built in memory of the Sufi saint, Nizam-ud-Din Chisti, who died in 1325. The tomb acquired the status of a shrine over the years, and today thousands of devotees visit the holy place to pray for the fulfillment of their wishes. Humayun's tomb, on which the Taj Mahal was later modelled, rests to the east of Nizam-ud-Din's shrine. It is the first mausoleum to be built in the centre of a garden divided into four squares. This tradition of 'charbagh' was

adopted by all Mughal monuments. The Purana Qila or Old Fort is to the north and encloses a mosque and the sixteenth-century Sher Mandal, a two-storeyed octagonal pavilion.

Within the beautiful Lodi Gardens to the west are some tombs and mosques that belong to the various Muslim dynasties, which established themselves prior to the Mughals. Safdarjung's Tomb of an early eighteenth century noble, near the Lodi Gardens, is equally well preserved. The need to surround their mausoleums with flower gardens and water channels was a regular feature of Muslim design and architecture.

While the mausoleums, monuments, forts and arches speak of the grandeur of Indo-Islamic rule, there is none to match the eloquent style of the Red Fort, situated on the bank of the River Yamuna beside the Jama Masjid, the chief mosque of Muslims in India.

The Red Fort or Qila Mubarak, as it was originally called, was planned as the residence and office of Emperor Shah Jahan. It was later used by the British as an army cantonment and armoury. The Fort was developed as a self-contained unit. The meticulous planning and detail, especially with regard to defense against possible enemy attack, and the fine expression of Mughal art, make a visit to the place mandatory. A moat surrounds the fort which was once filled by the Yamuna until the river

139

changed its course - an almost painful reminder of the decline of the all-powerful Mughals.

The Red Fort overlooks Chandni Chowk, an old market criss-crossed by a labyrinth of by-lanes renowned for their sweetmeats, crafts and traditional silver jewellery. Kinari Bazaar is a narrow colourful stretch of road that is truly exciting to wade through. The canal that divided the main thoroughfare once flowed with the waters of the River Yamuna. Along the main street, a dilapidated church still remains, the only remnant of a bygone era that has survived the passage of time. The main street is dotted with important places of worship. At the entrance is the Jain Temple that also boasts of a

bird hospital. A few steps away is the Gauri Shankar Temple dedicated to Lord Shiva, a holy place for the Hindus. Further down the street is an important Sikh shrine, Sish Ganj and next to the Gurudwara is a beautiful small mosque with golden domes aptly called the Sunehri Masjid.

To the north of the Red Fort is Metcalfe House, built in 1835 to house the British resident, and also St. James Church, built in 1824. The whole stretch between the church and the University of Delhi in the north is called Civil Lines. The place is filled with relics of the Raj and the earlier Mughal rule. The tombs, gardens and mosques, well over a hundred years old, stand evidence.

BELOW & OPPOSITE PAGE: THE KOHINOOR SUITE IN THE OBEROI, NEW DELHI, IS ULTRA CHIC, MODERN AND EXTREMELY COMFORTABLE; IT IS AIRY AND SPACIOUS, THUS GIVING ONE A SENSE OF ELATION; TEAK-PANELLED FLOOR OF THE BEDROOM GIVES IT A COZY AMBIENCE; IT IS SEPARATED BY A PASSAGE FROM THE DELIGHTFUL LIVING ROOM THAT IS FURNISHED WITH CHOICEST MARBLE AND DESIGNER FURNITURE AS SEEN ON THE OPPOSITE PAGE.

141

142

ABOVE: THE LATTICE WORK THAT DOMINATES THE FAR END OF THE LOBBY WAS INSPIRED FROM A MOSQUE IN AHMEDABAD; BONE-INLAID CHAIRS STAND ON EITHER SIDE OF THIS AMAZING WOODWORK. OPPOSITE PAGE: THE LOBBY IS A BEAUTIFUL BLEND OF TRADITION AND MODERNITY.

ABOVE, LEFT: LIVING ROOM OF LORD CURZON SUITE IN THE OBEROI, NEW DELHI. ABOVE, RIGHT: PORTRAIT OF A MUGHAL PRINCE DECORATES THE ENTRANCE LOBBY OF THE HOTEL. COLONIAL TABLE AND CHAIR PROVIDE PERFECT SETTING FOR THE ARTWORK. OPPOSITE PAGE: ANTIQUE WOODEN SCULPTURE OF CEREMONIAL BULL STANDS GUARD IN THE CORNER. AN ANTIQUE PORTUGUESE STYLE CUPBOARD FROM GOA STANDS IN THE CENTRE, DIVIDING THE LIVING AND THE BEDROOM AREAS.

ABOVE, LEFT: INFORMAL SEATING AREA OF THE KOHINOOR SUITE IS WELL APPOINTED WITH LUXURIOUS HAND TUFT RUGS AND LEATHER ARMCHAIRS. ABOVE, RIGHT: SCENTED CANDLES LINE UP THE WALL OF THE CITY'S LATEST SPA. OPPOSITE PAGE: LUXURIES OF THE KOHINOOR SUITE DON'T JUST END IN THE LIVING ROOM AND THE BEDROOM BUT EVEN EXTEND TO THE BATHROOM. FULL GLASS WALLS PROVIDE UNINTERRUPTED VIEWS OF THE ADJOINING GOLF GREENS. THE TEAK WOOD FLOOR CONTINUES ONTO PRIVATE MASSAGE ROOM IN THE FAR END.

149

BELOW: THE WELL-STOCKED BAR OF '360 DEGREE' IS A POPULAR PLACE TO ENJOY THE FINEST WINES AND SPIRITS. OPPOSITE PAGE: THE PRIVATE DINING AREA OF THE RESTAURANT CAN BE SEEN. FOLLOWING PAGES: CLUB BAR OF THE OBEROI, NEW DELHI, IS SPACIOUS AND COMFORTABLE, A PERFECT PLACE TO HAVE A BUSINESS MEETING; LARGE WINDOWS BATHE IT IN NATURAL LIGHT THROUGHOUT THE DAY.

151

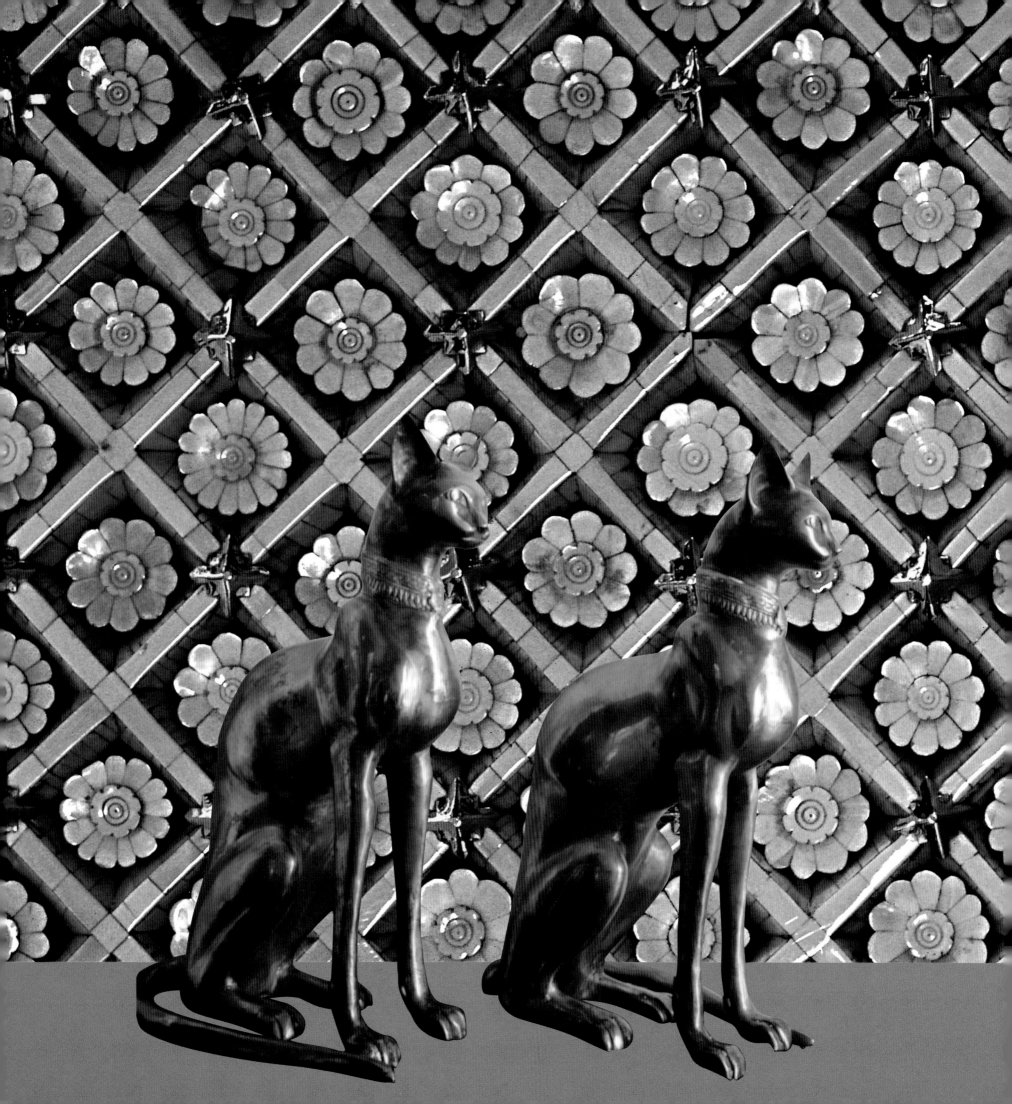

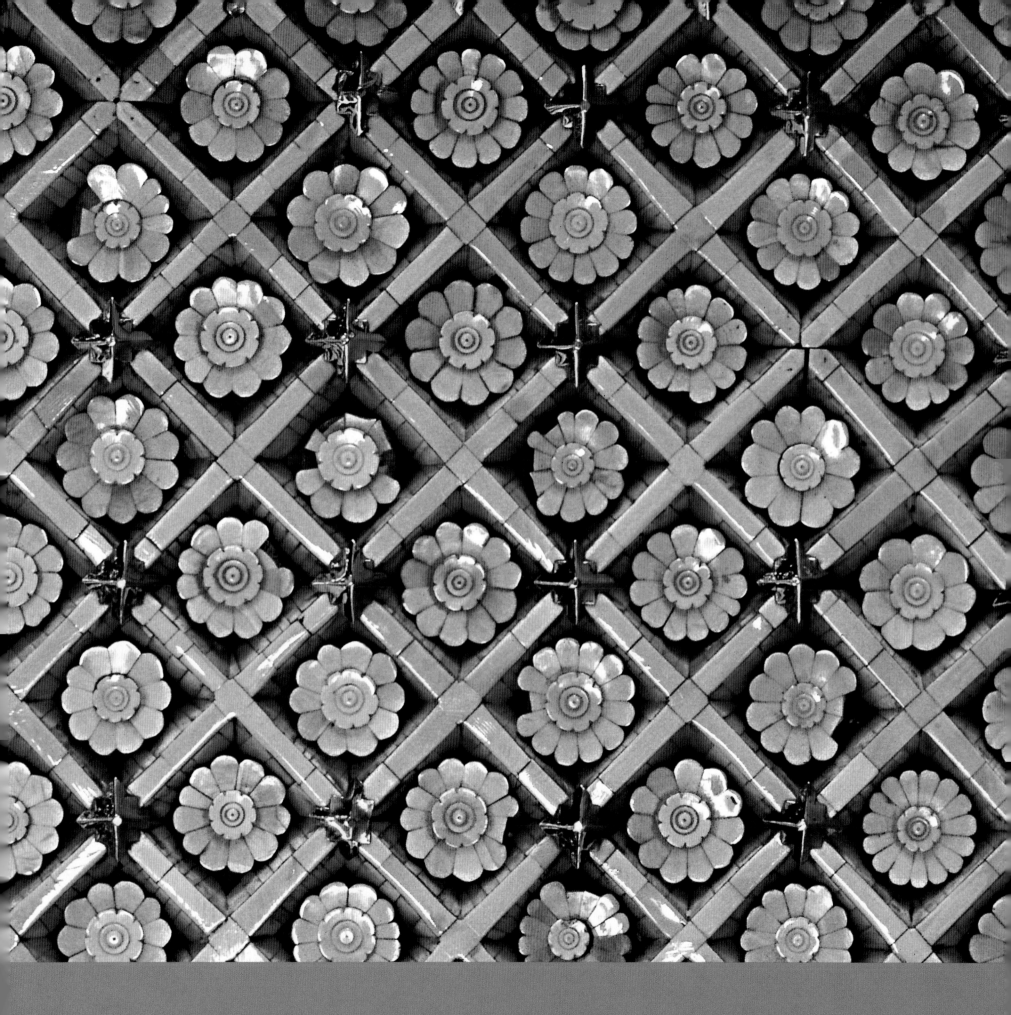

MUMBAI

156

Bombay (now Mumbai), apparently the busiest city of India, is also the financial capital of the country, popular for its film industry and the infamous underworld. The city and its buildings may look in a constant state of decay but the city pays 40% of India's total taxes.

Today, this city, which is less than 500 years old since it was discovered by the Portuguese, has metamorphosed into a sprawling megalopolis of 14 million people. It does not have a distinct regional character because of its mixed population. The separate identity that each community maintains has given the city a blend of places of worship, customs and rituals, making it very cosmopolitan in character.

In 1996, Bombay was renamed Mumbai, which is the Marathi name of a local deity. It is also the film capital of India with the largest film industry in the world. Over a thousand movies are made in India annually, in which majority make losses but still the lure of glitz and glamour draws thousands to this industry.

Mumbai originally consisted of seven islands inhabited by small Koli fishing communities. The Portuguese handed the largest island of Bom Bain (Good Bay) to the English in 1661, as part of Catherine of Braganza's dowry

when she married Charles II. A few years later, in 1668, it was leased out to the East India Company for a pittance. The city grew in importance with the opening of the railways in the nineteenth century, and its natural harbour became an international port of call with the construction of the Suez Canal in 1869. The Civil War in America caused the cotton supplies to shrink in the world market. This proved to be a boon in disguise for the city. Trade boomed as the city was located close to the cotton-producing region and had a natural port to boast of. The Gothic buildings that dominate Mumbai's skyline date back to this period.

Subsequently, Mumbai rapidly became the centre of an entrepreneurial as well as a commercial class, drawing from the Parsis as well as Bania and Gujarati business community. The small Parsi community has been instrumental in the development of the Indian industry. The Tatas are a household name in India. The family gave Mumbai its landmark, the Taj Mahal Hotel. Built in Edwardian style by Chambers in 1903, it is still regarded as one of the finest hotels of the world.

Besides the Maharashtrian, Gujarati and Christian communities, there is also a small minority of Jews in Mumbai. Unlike Delhi, which is dotted with the

ruins of Muslim dynasties, it is the British landmarks that stand out in Mumbai. Prime among them is the Gateway of India which was designed by George Wittet to commemorate the visit of King George V and Queen Mary in 1911. Ironically, it was through this very arch that the last contingent of British troops (1st Battalion Somerset Light Infantry) in India left by sea in 1948. Wittet also designed the Prince of Wales Museum, which houses a pot-pourrie of Indian, European and Far Eastern artefacts.

The Victoria Terminus, popularly known as VT, was built in the last quarter of the nineteenth century by F.W. Stevens. It is a truly remarkable Victorian-Gothic style building. The numerous sculptures decorating its façade were designed by Thomas Earp and executed by the students of the Arts College. A visit to the Victoria Terminus gives one a taste of the pulsating energy of the city. Every working day, nearly four million people come to work in the city from far-off suburbs using the local trains. Other colonial buildings include Old Secretariat, Crawford Market and the Municipal Building.

More than the architecture, it is the sea which surrounds the city on three sides that dominates the cultural consciousness of the city and dictates its lifestyle. Beaches and seaside promenades like Marine Drive, Chowpati and

BELOW: THE ELEPHANTA CAVE, DATING BACK TO THE 7TH CENTURY, IS A GROUP OF ROCK-CUT TEMPLES DEDICATED TO LORD SHIVA. AN HOUR'S RIDE FROM THE GATEWAY OF INDIA TAKES YOU TO THIS WORLD HERITAGE SITE. OPPOSITE PAGE: BOMBAY UNIVERSITY BUILDING, A BEAUTIFUL GOTHIC ARCHITECTURE, AND THE VICTORIA TERMINUS ARE AMONG MANY COLONIAL MONUMENTS THAT DOT THE CITYSCAPE. PREVIOUS PAGES: THE GATEWAY OF INDIA IS THE HISTORIC LANDMARK OF THE CITY THAT WAS BUILT TO RECEIVE THE BRITISH CROWN ON THEIR VISIT TO INDIA. THIS WAS THE VERY PLACE FROM WHERE THE LAST OF THE BRITISH TROOPS LEFT AFTER INDEPENDENCE.

Juhu beach, though eaten into by the urban expansion, are still a visitor's delight. The beaches are used not for swimming but for enjoying the rather famous and spicy bhel puri snack or for political and religious gatherings.

Mumbai is also the boarding point for the Elephanta Caves ferry ride. This enchanting island, an hour away by motor launch, offers a welcome getaway from the chaos of the bustling city. There are a series of beautiful rock-cut caves with temples and sculptures dating back to the sixth century. The island was named by the Portuguese in honour of the carved elephant they found at the port. Its chief attraction is a unique cave temple, which houses a six-metre high bust of Shiva in his three manifestations as the Creator, Preserver and Destroyer (Brahma, Vishnu and Mahesh) of the universe.

Mumbai is the most prosperous city in the country, with a cost of living almost equal to that in the U.S. The city houses some of the most expensive properties in the world. However, poverty continues to be a growing vice with one-third of Mumbai's population living in slums or shanty towns. Despite communal tensions and a growing mafia nexus posing a grave threat to the city, Mumbai maintains its status as the financial, commercial and entertainment capital of India.

THE MAGNIFICENT ATRIUM LOBBY OF **THE OBEROI, MUMBAI** IS SPLENDIDLY COVERED WITH GRANITE AND PUNCTUATED WITH MODERN SCULPTURES AND FRESH FLOWERS; LARGE WINDOWS PROVIDE FABULOUS VISTAS OF THE BAY WHILE THE MELLOW NOTES FROM THE PIANO FILL THE AIR.

ABOVE & OPPOSITE PAGE: THE KOHINOOR SUITE OF THE OBEROI, MUMBAI OCCUPIES THE CORNER OF THE TOP FLOOR OF THE HOTEL. ITS LARGE WINDOWS PROVIDE UNINTERRUPTED VIEWS OF THE ARABIAN SEA AND THE PICTURESQUE MARINE DRIVE.

BELOW: MARINE DRIVE LOOKS BEAUTIFUL AT DAWN FROM THE KOHINOOR SUITE OF THE OBEROI, MUMBAI. OPPOSITE PAGE: GUEST ROOMS IN THE OBEROI, MUMBAI PROVIDE SPLENDID VIEWS OF THE ARABIAN SEA.

ABOVE: 'TIFFIN' RESTAURANT, LOCATED ON THE LOBBY LEVEL, HAS AN INFORMAL, RELAXED AMBIENCE AND SERVES MULTI-CUISINE DISHES ROUND THE CLOCK. OPPOSITE PAGE: STRIKING FLOWER DECORATION IN 'VECTOR' RESTAURANT.

SHIMLA

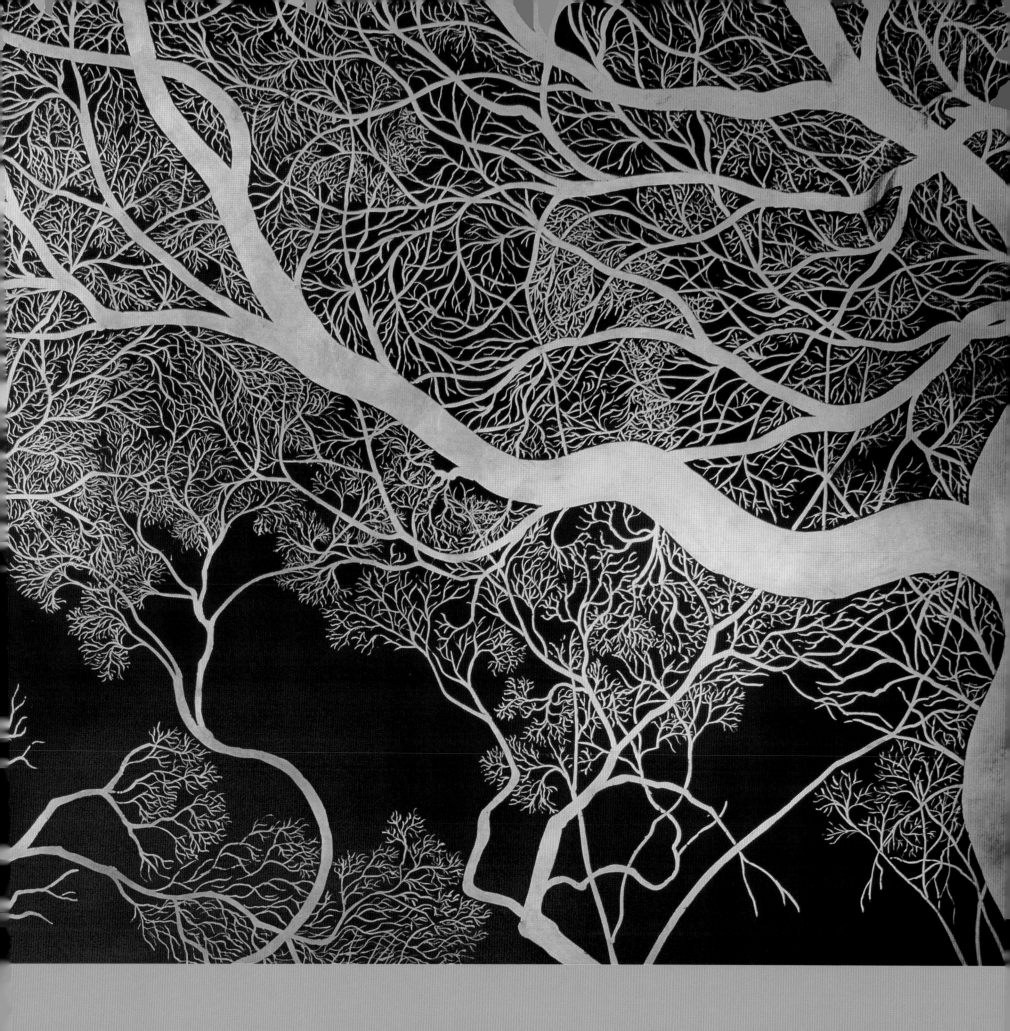

Shimla derives its name from the local goddess, Shimla, an incarnation of Kali. This picturesque town situated at 7000 feet is surrounded by pine, oak, deodar and rhododendron forest. Shimla, the capital of Himachal Pradesh, was built by the Scottish civil servant Charles Pratt Kennedy as the first British summer home in 1822, and by the latter half of the 19th century, the town had become the summer capital of the British Raj. British soldiers, merchants, and civil servants moved there every year to escape the heat and dust of the Indo-Gangetic plain. Today, the hill station is thronged by Indian and foreign tourists and has become an important honeymoon destination of North India. Imposing Victorian monuments of the Raj are still the highlights of the summer capital.

The fresh Himalayan air seems scented with cedar and pine trees that line along the few roads that are in this town. Not permitting vehicular traffic, adds to the charm of aimlessly rambling in the mall. Since British times, Shimla has been known for its residential schools. Of them, the Bishop Cotton School is perhaps the best known. Founded in 1859, Bishop Cotton was originally established to educate the children of British Army officers. The school's alumni have distinguished themselves in every sphere of public life, though General Michael O'Dwyer, the British officer who ordered the Jallianwala Bagh massacre, remains its most infamous student.

The heritage Kalka-Shimla Railway, popularly known as the toy train, runs on narrow gauge (76-metres wide) railway line. The train speed is slow but the scenic beauty and the 103 big and small tunnels en route make the journey memorable.

The ridge and the adjacent Mall form the heart of Shimla. Vehicular traffic is not allowed along the Mall, making it a favourite place for taking a brisk walk. This is also the main shopping area with most of the shops still housed in old traditional British buildings. One tier below this shopping area is the Middle Bazaar with smaller shops mixed with residences. A tier below Middle Bazaar is the Lower Bazaar which houses small

shops catering to everyday needs and the vegetable market called the Sabzi Mandi. This market is the most crowded of the three though the going can get tough on the Mall Road during peak tourist season. Most of the locals shop from the Lower Bazaar, using the Mall Road to shop for durables.

There are many interesting Raj relics to be seen in Shimla. Gaiety Theatre on the Mall Road is one of them. It opened on the 30th of May 1887 to commemorate Queen Victoria's Jubilee Year. It is an architectural marvel of the Raj and continues the tradition of holding English plays over the weekend. This theatre has always been the hub of all cultural activities

of Shimla. Many of the actors who performed here later went on to make impression in West End, Broadway and of course, Bollywood. Notable personalities like Lord Kitchner, Mrs. Deane, Rudyard Kipling and Sir Dennis Fitz Patrick were associated with this theatre.

On the Observatory Hills is the Vice Regal Lodge. It was formerly the summer residence of the British Viceroys. It is an imposing British Raj style mansion that was built under the supervision of Lord Dufferin in 1888. The teak panelled halls and few rooms are open to the public; rest of the lodge is reserved for the research and writers in residence.

Christ Church, built in 1884, is one of the earliest churches to be built in India. Lockwood Kipling, father of Rudyard Kipling, executed the frescoes that surround the chapel. The stain glass windows and the organ are important attractions of this famous landmark of Shimla.

Right next to the Christ Church is a beautiful, small Elizabethan style building that is known as the Library. It was built in 1910 by James Ransome, a British civil engineer.

A 45-minute drive takes you from Shimla to the Wildflower Resort in Mashobra. The building was originally conceived by Lord Kitchner in 1902 as a getaway from the crowded party life of the British summer capital. It was converted into a modest hotel in 1925. This building was charred in

a fire in the 1990s which gave the new owners an opportunity to make the best resort hotel in the Himalayas. Wildflower Hall is situated at 8,350 feet in the magnificent Himalayas. It is a fairytale luxury resort set in 23 acres of virgin woods of pine and cedar. The resort boasts of all weather heated swimming pools that are enclosed by floor-to-ceiling glass panes that provide an uninterrupted view of the Himalayas. There is also an outdoor hot pool on the deck to soak in the beauty of pinewood forest and the Himalayas.

Trekking along the jungle trails in thick pine wood forest around Wildflower Hall, one can soak in the natural virgin beauty of the mighty Himalayas. There is a fabulous variety of flora and fauna for the nature enthusiast's short walks from the resort. For the rush of adrenalin, one can indulge in white water rafting in the River Sutlej or go for a horse ride along the mountain trail with sumptuous picnic basket in tow. From the inside, the resort is lavishly decorated with teak wood panelling on the floor as well as on the walls. The rich leather armchairs sit on the finest hand-knotted carpets, while mahogany tables and lounge chairs capture the ambience and essence of the Colonial era.

It is often said that Wildflower Hall is the shortest road to heaven via the Himalayas and, believe me, it is true in every sense of the word.

181

ABOVE, LEFT: THE VIEW OF THE RESORT FROM THE GAZEBO IN THE FRONT GARDEN. **ABOVE, RIGHT:** THE TERRACE OUTSIDE THE COFFEE SHOP HAS THE BACKDROP OF THICK PINE WOOD, MAKING IT A PERFECT SETTING FOR MEALS. **OPPOSITE PAGE:** THE HEATED PLUNGE POOL IS AN ABSOLUTE LUXURY; IT PROVIDES BREATHTAKING VIEWS OF THE VALLEY AND THE HIMALAYAS BEYOND, A PERFECT PLACE TO SOAK IN THE ELEMENTS OF NATURE. **FOLLOWING PAGES:** THE HIGHLIGHT OF THIS HIMALAYAN RESORT IS THE SWIMMING POOL. IT IS ENCLOSED BY FLOOR TO CEILING GLASS THAT PROVIDES UNINTERRUPTED VIEWS OF THE SURROUNDING VALLEY WHILE MAINTAINING THE AIR-CONDITIONED COMFORT. HUGE CRYSTAL CHANDELIERS HANG FROM THE CEILING TO LEND IT AN AIR OF EXTRAVAGANCE; MOSAIC OF FLORAL MOTIFS SURROUNDS THIS ALL WEATHER HEATED POOL.

187

ABOVE, LEFT & OPPOSITE PAGE: THE HIMALAYAN RESORT BOASTS OF A VARIETY OF ACTIVITIES BOTH INDOOR AND OUTDOOR. THE POOL TABLE AND SCRABBLE ARE AMONG THE MANY CHOICES AVAILABLE. ABOVE, RIGHT: LORD KITCHNER BUILT WILDFLOWER HALL, SHIMLA IN THE HIMALAYAS IN 1902. HIS PHOTOGRAPHS DECORATE THE MANTLEPIECE OF THE FIRE-PLACE IN THE LORD KITCHNER SUITE.

189

BELOW: MULTIPLE DINING CHOICES ARE AVAILABLE FOR THE GUESTS IN THE VARIETY OF RESTAURANTS IN WILDFLOWER HALL, SHIMLA IN THE HIMALAYAS. OPPOSITE PAGE: LORD KITCHNER'S PORTRAIT HANGS OVER THE FIREPLACE IN THE TEAK WOOD PANELLED LOBBY; ANTIQUE PERSIAN CARPETS COVER THE ENTIRE FLOOR.

193

ABOVE: DECK CHAIRS ARE ARRANGED INVITINGLY FOR THE GUESTS TO LOUNGE AROUND THE LUXURIOUS POOL OF THIS HIMALAYAN RESORT. OPPOSITE PAGE: NATURAL LIGHT FLOODS THE COFFEE SHOP MAKING IT A LIVELY ROOM FOR BREAKFAST. PERIOD PHOTOGRAPHS OF THE EARLY 1900s BRITISH GENTRY DECORATE THE WALLS. FOLLOWING PAGE: VICEREGAL LODGE WAS FORMERLY THE SUMMER RESIDENCE OF THE BRITISH VICEROYS. IT IS AN IMPOSING BRITISH RAJ STYLE MANSION THAT WAS BUILT UNDER THE SUPERVISION OF LORD DUFFERIN IN 1888.

ABOVE: TEAK WOOD PANELLING AND BANISTERS ARE USED LIBERALLY IN THE CONSTRUCTION OF THE OBEROI CECIL, SHIMLA. OPPOSITE PAGE: ATRIUM LOBBY OF THE OBEROI CECIL, SHIMLA IS BRIGHTLY LIT WITH THE GLASS ROOF. THE WELL-STOCKED BAR STANDS AT THE FAR END OF THE HALL AND PLUSH LEATHER CHAIRS ARE ARRANGED AROUND SMALL TABLES ON THE TEAK WOOD FLOOR; A HAND-KNOTTED PERSIAN CARPET LOOKS DRAMATIC IN THE CENTRE.

ABOVE: THE ROOMS IN THE OBEROI CECIL, SHIMLA ARE WELL APPOINTED AND COMFORTABLE. CHOICEST MATERIALS WERE HAND-PICKED TO RETAIN THE FLAVOUR OF ITS COLONIAL OPULENCE. OPPOSITE PAGE: DETAILS OF THE HAND-CARVED MARBLE ARTEFACTS WITH FRESH FLOWERS DECORATE THE PUBLIC AREAS OF WILDFLOWER HALL, SHIMLA IN THE HIMALAYAS.

ABOVE: THE POOL IN WILDFLOWER HALL, SHIMLA IN THE HIMALAYAS IS ENCLOSED WITH HIGH GLASS WINDOWS THAT KEEP THE CHILL OUT BUT NOT THE STUNNING VISTAS. OPPOSITE PAGE: THE ALL WEATHER HEATED POOL IN THE OBEROI CECIL, SHIMLA RETAINS ITS COLONIAL CHARM - A PERFECT PLACE TO LEAF THROUGH THE RAJ LITERATURE.

CALCUTTA

204

Calcutta (now Kolkata) is located in eastern India on the banks of the River Hooghly. The name was probably based on Kalikata, one of the three villages in the area before the arrival of the British. The city served as the capital of India during the British Raj until 1911 when the capital was transferred to Delhi.

Calcutta's history begins with the arrival of the British East India Company in 1690. Job Charnock, an administrator with the Company, is traditionally credited as the founder of this city. In 1699, the British completed the construction of old Fort William, which was used to station its troops and as a regional base. Calcutta was declared a Presidency City, and later became the headquarters of the Bengal Presidency. Faced with frequent skirmishes with French forces in 1756, the British began to upgrade their fortifications. When protests against the militarization by the Nawab of Bengal Siraj-Ud-Daulah went unheeded, he attacked and captured Fort William, leading to the infamous Black Hole incident. A force of Company sepoys and British troops led by Robert Clive recaptured the city the following year. Calcutta was named the capital of British India in 1772. It was during this period that the marshes surrounding the city were drained and

the government area was laid out along the banks of the Hooghly River. Richard Wellesley, the Governor General between 1797 and 1805, was largely responsible for the growth of the city and its public architecture which led to the description of Kolkata as 'The City of Palaces'.

The city was a centre of the British East India Company's opium trade during the 18th and 19th century. The company would buy opium from local traders and farmers and sell it at auction in Calcutta, from where much of it was smuggled to Canton in China, eventually leading to the Opium Wars between Britain and China.

The city underwent rapid industrial growth from the 1850s, especially in the textile and jute sectors; this caused a massive investment in infrastructure projects like rail, roads and telegraph by British government. The coalescence of British and Indian culture resulted in the emergence of a new Babu class of urbane Indians whose members were often Anglophiles professionals employed by the British. Throughout the nineteenth century, a socio-cultural reform – often referred to as the Bengal Renaissance – resulted in the general uplifting of the people. Calcutta became a centre of the Indian Independence movement.

In the mid-1980s, Bombay (now Mumbai) overtook Calcutta as India's most populous city. Calcutta has been a strong base of Indian communism and has been ruled by the Left Front for three decades now — the world's longest-running 'democratically-elected' Communist government.

The city is the main business, commercial and financial hub of eastern India and the north-eastern states. It is home to the Calcutta Stock Exchange, India's second-largest bourse. It is also a major commercial and military port, and the only city in the region to have an international airport. Once India's leading city and capital, Calcutta experienced a steady economic decline in the years following India's Independence due to the prevalent unstabilized political condition and rise in trade unionism supported by left-wing parties. Between the 1960s to the mid-1990s, flight of capital was enormous as many large factories were closed or downsized and businesses relocated. The lack of capital and resources coupled with a worldwide glut in demand in the city's traditional industries (e.g., jute) added to the depressed state of the city's economy. The liberalisation of the Indian economy in the 1990s brought in improvement in the city's fortunes.

In some areas of the city, hand-pulled rickshaws are also patronised

by the public for short distances. Kolkata has long been known for its literary, artistic and revolutionary heritage. The city was the birthplace of modern Indian literary and artistic thought. Kolkatans tend to have a special appreciation for art and literature; it is evident from the number of art shows that are held and theatre groups that exist in the city. A characteristic feature of Kolkata is the Para or neighbourhoods having a strong sense of community. Typically, every Para has its own community club with a clubroom and, often, a playing field. People here habitually indulge in adda or leisurely chat, and these adda sessions are often a form of free-style intellectual conversation. The city has a tradition of political graffiti depicting everything from outrageous slander to witty banter and limericks, caricatures to propaganda.

The city has a tradition of dramas in the form of jatra (a kind of folk-theatre), and group theatres. Kolkata is known for its Bengali cinema industry, with Kolkatans having special affection for the legendary actor Uttam Kumar, and for parallel cinema. Its long tradition of filmmaking includes acclaimed directors like Satyajit Ray. The city is also noted for its rich literary tradition set by Rabindranath Tagore, who was awarded

BELOW: FLOWER MARKET AT THE BASE OF THE HOWRAH BRIDGE IS A SPECTACULAR PLACE TO SEE THE RIOT OF COLOURS AND THE ENERGY INVOLVED IN THE TRADING OF FLOWERS, WHICH ARE USED DURING EVERY OCCASION IN DAILY LIFE.

the Nobel Prize for Literature, Sarat Chandra, and many others.

Another famous Kolkatan was Mother Teresa. She gained worldwide acclaim with her tireless efforts on behalf of working with the poorest of the poor. Her work brought her numerous humanitarian awards, including the Pope John XXIII Peace Prize and the Nobel Peace Prize in 1979. In receiving this award, Mother Teresa revolutionized the award ceremony. She insisted on a departure from the ceremonial banquet and asked that the funds ($ 6000) be donated to the poor in Kolkata. This money would permit her to feed hundreds for a year. Kolkata has many buildings adorned with Gothic,

Baroque, Roman, Oriental and Indo-Islamic (including Mughal) motifs. The city is dotted with colonial buildings which are best explored on foot. The Indian Museum (the oldest museum in Asia) established in 1814 and the Victoria Memorial, are the major tourist attractions in Kolkata. The Victoria Memorial was built between 1906 and 1921. It is a majestic white marble building at the southern end of the Maidan surrounded by a sprawling garden. A black bronze Angel of Victory, holding a bugle in her hand was placed at the apex of the dome above the Memorial. It is fixed to its pedestal with ball bearings and acts as a weathercock when the wind is strong enough.

209

It was designed by Sir William Emerson in an architectural style similar to Belfast City Hall. Although he was asked to design the building in the Italian Renaissance style, Emerson incorporated Mughal elements in the structure.

Durga Puja is the most notable of all the religious and social festivals in Kolkata. It occurs over a period of nine days in October. 'Kumar Tuli' or the artists' village is an interesting area to explore. Here one can see hundreds of artisans giving shape to the statues of the various Hindu deities, using only straw and clay. These statues are dried in the sun, painted and decorated with all the finery deserved by the Almighty. Various religious associations from across the city buy them for communal worship; after worshipping for nearly over a week, the statues are taken to the river bank among much fanfare and then immersed in the waters of River Hooghly.

Another place worth a visit is the flower market. It is picturesquely located on the bank of river Hooghly, under the Howrah Bridge. Tons of flowers are brought to the market from the countryside everyday and are sold by kilos. These are used in religious ceremonies or on festive occasions like weddings. The kaleidoscope of colours and the frenzy of the market make the visit a rewarding experience.

THE OBEROI GRAND IS THE HISTORIC LANDMARK OF CALCUTTA. IT STILL RETAINS ITS COLONIAL CHARM WITHOUT SACRIFICING THE MODERN COMFORTS. **OPPOSITE PAGE:** THE ENTRANCE PORCH OF THE HOTEL. **BELOW:** THE FAÇADE OF THE HOTEL REFLECTS INTO THE SHIMMERING POOL.

BELOW: THE LOBBY OF THE OBEROI GRAND, CALCUTTA IS ILLUMINATED WITH AN ANTIQUE CRYSTAL CHANDELIER; THE GRECIAN COLUMNS IN THE CORNER ARE GILDED. OPPOSITE PAGE: THE GUEST ROOMS ARE SPACIOUS AND WELL APPOINTED WITH LARGE WINDOWS OVERLOOKING THE POOL; CHOICEST CARPETS, SILK AND LINEN FURNISHING, AND COLONIAL FOUR-POSTER BEDS ARE USED TO EMBELLISH THE ROOMS.

ABOVE: THE SPECTACULAR VIEW OF THE LOBBY GREETS YOU AS YOU ENTER **THE OBEROI GRAND, CALCUTTA**; THE FLOOR IS LAID OUT IN UDAIPUR GREEN MARBLE INLAID WITH WHITE MARBLE SQUARES; ANTIQUE PERSIAN RUGS COVER THE FLOOR; THE SOFAS ARE FURNISHED WITH FRENCH TAPESTRY AND INDIAN SILKS ADORN THE CUSHIONS; CRYSTAL VASES WITH COLOURED FLOWERS BRIGHTEN UP THE AREA. **OPPOSITE PAGE:** THE EXTRAVAGANT BALLROOM IS AN ENGINEERING MARVEL AS IT IS NOT SUPPORTED BY ANY COLUMN; IT HAS BEEN THE VENUE FOR THE MOST IMPORTANT EVENTS OF THE CITY.

BANGALORE

BELOW: The 8th-century Durga Temple is the main attraction of the sleepy village of Aihole. The temple is apsidal in plan, along the lines of a Buddhist chaitya. A pillared corridor with beautiful carvings of the Hindu divinities envelops the shrine. **Opposite page:** Early 12th-century Chennakeshava Temple at Belur, is dedicated to the 'handsome Vishnu' in north Karnataka. Legend has it that it took 103 years to complete, which is not surprising as the façade of the temple is filled with intricate sculptures and friezes; a giant temple chariot is being decorated for the festivities.

Bangalore (now Bengaluru) is the fifth largest metro in India with its population close to six million. Great Kannada warrior, Kempe Gowda, laid the foundation of the city in 1537 declaring it as a province of Vijayanagar Empire. After the fall of the Vijayanagar Empire, it was captured by the Marathas who eventually sold Bangalore in the year 1687 to the Maharaja of Mysore for a princely sum of Rs. 300,000. Later, after the passing away of Krishnaraja Wodeyar II in 1759, Hyder Ali, Commander-in-Chief of Mysore forces, proclaimed himself as the ruler of Mysore. After Hyder Ali's death, his son, Tipu Sultan, also known as the 'Tiger of Mysore,' ruled the region. In 1799, British East India Company's forces defeated Tipu Sultan and returned the control of Bangalore to the Wodeyars. However, they retained the control of the cantonment area of the city. In 1831, the capital of Mysore state was transferred from Mysore to Bangalore. Bangalore's reputation as the Garden City of India began in 1927 with the Silver Jubilee celebrations of the rule of Krishnaraja Wodeyar IV. Several projects such as the construction of parks, public buildings and hospitals were instituted to beautify the city. After Indian Independence in August 1947, Bangalore remained in the new Mysore State of which the Maharaja of Mysore was the 'Rajpramukh.'

Today, the city is going through an unprecedented economic boom. Its businesses are attracting young professionals, not only from India but from

BELOW: THE PALACE OF MYSORE WAS THE OFFICIAL RESIDENCE OF THE WODEYAR DYNASTY, THE FORMER ROYAL FAMILY OF MYSORE. THE ARCHITECTURAL STYLE IS INDO-SARACENIC THAT BEAUTIFULLY BLENDS HINDU, MUSLIM, RAJPUT, AND GOTHIC STYLES OF ARCHITECTURE. THE PALACE MADE OF GREY GRANITE WITH DEEP PINK MARBLE DOMES WAS DESIGNED BY HENRY IRWIN IN 1912. **OPPOSITE PAGE:** LALIT MAHAL PALACE IS SITUATED JUST OUTSIDE MYSORE AND STANDS AS A SHIMMERING WHITE ITALIAN PALAZZO, SET IN SPRAWLING TERRACED AND LANDSCAPED GARDENS. IT WAS BUILT IN 1931 BY THE ERSTWHILE MAHARAJA OF MYSORE TO HOST THE VICEROY OF INDIA.

all over the world. Because of the high disposable incomes of the young workforce, there has been mushrooming of pubs, fancy restaurants and the entertainment industry with international rock bands performing here.

Much of the credit for this transformation of Bangalore goes to industrial visionaries like Sir Mirza Ismail and Sir Mokshagundam Visvesvaraya who in the 1940s played a pivotal role in the development of Bangalore's manufacturing and industrial growth. The rapid growth of Information Technology has made Bangalore the software capital of the country. Many MNC's have established their base here. But this has put pressure on its poor infrastructure and led to tensions between IT professionals and the laidback bureaucracy which has its electoral base in rural Karnataka.

Biotechnology is a rapidly expanding field in the city. Bangalore accounts for 47% of the biotechnology companies in India. Aeronautics and scientific research are other major areas that have catered to the diversified growth of the city.

Bangalore is also known as the 'Garden City of India' because of its climate, greenery and the presence of many public parks. Another unique feature of the city is that the weather remains cool throughout the year. This is unlike other cities of the South that remain hot, hotter or hottest!

The city is a perfect launch pad for the excursions deeper into Karnataka.

Mysore, with the Palace of the Maharaja, continues to be the centre of cultural life in Karnataka. Henry Irwin built the palace in an Indo-Saracenic style of grand proportions in 1912, for Maharaja Krishnaraja Wadiyar IV. It is one of the largest palaces in the country, beautifully restored and maintained. The Palace hosts the world famous Dussehra festival every year in the month of October. The former princely state of Mysore is also famous for its sandalwood and jasmine gardens.

The majestic Elephant Gate is the main entrance to the centre of the palace and bears the Mysore royal symbol of the double-headed eagle, now the state emblem. The elaborately decorated, gem-studded elephant howda,

made of 84 kg gold, is of particular interest and is used to carry the deity during the Dussehra festival.

The octagonal Kalyan Mandap, the royal wedding hall south of the courtyard, has a beautiful stained glass ceiling and magnificently detailed oil paintings illustrating the great Mysore Dussehra festival of 1930. This opulent hall still houses some of the finest Belgian crystal, silver furniture and Bohemian chandeliers.

An Italian marble staircase leads to the magnificent Darbar Hall, a grand colonnaded hall with lavishly framed paintings by famous Indian artists including Raja Ravi Varma. The massive hall affords views across the parade

ground and gardens to Chamundi Hill. The Maharaja gave audience from here, seated on a throne made from 280 kg of solid Karnatakan gold.

The passage through the beautifully inlaid wood and ivory door of the Ganesh Temple leads to the Ambavilas, the private audience hall. This extraordinary decorated hall features beautiful stained glass and gold leaf paintings.

Three richly decorated doors lead to the Diwan-i-Khas. The central silver door depicts Vishnu's ten incarnations and the eight Dikpalas or the directional guardians.

The Jaganmohan Palace, a little further west of the Maharaja's palace, was used as a royal residence until Krishnaraja Wadiyar IV turned it into a

picture gallery and museum in 1915. The ground floor displays costumes, musical instruments and numerous portraits and photographs. A series of nineteenth and twentieth century paintings dominate the first floor. The work of Raja Ravi Varma is particularly interesting, because he was first to introduce modern techniques in Indian art.

Devraja market is a tourist's delight. It has numerous stalls selling fruits, vegetables, colourful kumkum used by Hindu women in the parting of their hair to announce their marital status, and jasmine flowers being sold by the kilos. Incense and spice shops abound this colourful marketplace.

Chamundi Hill, immediately to the south-east of the city, is topped with

a temple of Durga Chamundeshwari, the chosen deity of the Mysore Rajas. This 12th-century temple features a Chamundi figure of solid gold. Outside in the courtyard, stands a fearsome statue of the demon buffalo, Mahishasur. A little further downhill is a magnificent five-metre high Nandi, Shiva's bull, which dates back to the seventeenth century.

The Hoysalas, who were the feudal lords of the Chalukyas of Kalyani, became independent in the eleventh century and founded a new dynasty with their name. They constructed magnificent temples in Halebid, Belur and Somnathpur. Hoysala temples stand out more for their sculptural workmanship rather than architectural achievements.

The three temples of Halebid, Belur and Somnathpur, situated in the state of Karnataka, are considered the gems of Hoysala architecture. The hallmarks of these temples are the star-shaped platforms with wide circumambulatory space on which they are built.

The Hoysala temple consists of a vimana, connected by a short antrala to a closed navaranga that is succeeded by mandapa. The temple walls have many triangular folds, which gave artists more surface area to exhibit their skills on, and also the play of light and shadow is thus more amplified. The carvings are so fine and delicate that at the first glance they appear to have been done on sandalwood. Nowhere in India are temples so intricately

carved as are these three. Every square inch of their walls is lavishly decorated with figures of gods and goddesses, along with an elaborate foliage design
on each divinity. The remaining surface is covered with Hindu epics like
Mahabharata and Ramayana. Armies of soldiers and animals cover the lower
part of the temple. Another noteworthy feature is the lathe-turned columns,
which adorn the temple hall and circumventor passages.

The temples were built between the twelfth and thirteenth century by the
Hoysala dynasty. The origin of the name of the dynasty is a heroic legend in
which Sala, the founder of the dynasty, kills a tiger single-handedly. This story
can be seen translated into a sculpture of Sala fighting the tiger at all
temples. Unlike other temples of India that are made out of granite or
sandstone, Hoysala temples are made with softer dark grey-green chlorite
schist, which is conducive to fine carving and hardens with the passage of
time. No wonder the details of the sculptures are simply exquisite. So minute
are the carvings that even the details such as jewellery worn by the divinities,
the rings on the fingers, the nails, or, as in one statue, the bracelet of the
dancer is free to rotate on her wrist. After the destruction of Halebid at the
hands of the Muslims, a new capital Belur was established close by.

The early 12th-century Chennakeshava Temple at Belur is dedicated to the 'handsome Vishnu'. Legend has it that it took 103 years to complete, which is not surprising as the façade of the temple is filled with intricate sculptures and friezes. If there were a competition among the most exotic sights of India, Hampi would be a serious contender for the first place. This city of victory, Vijayanagara, is set in a surreal landscape of large smooth boulders that have miraculously hung in balance through centuries. In this awesome theatre of nature are the ruins of Vijayanagara, spread in an area of twenty-six square kilometres. The history of the site gains importance with the Vijayanagara Dynasty in the fourteenth century. Two brothers, Harihara and Bukka, laid the foundation of the empire in 1336. Later, Bukka's son, Harihara II, not only consolidated the empire but also brought Sri Lanka and Burma under Vijayanagara's control. Later, in the early sixteenth century, Vijayanagara entered its golden era under the rule of Krishnadevaraya. He had visitors from Persia, Italy and Portugal at his court. All of them speak of the splendours of his empire and the affluence of its citizens. It is not hard to imagine the splendour of Hampi by the magnitude of ruins that still abound the site.

229

BELOW: THE LILY POOL SURROUNDING THE THAI PAVILION LENDS AN ENCHANTING SENSE OF TROPICAL LOCATION. OPPOSITE PAGE: THE PATIO OUTSIDE THE BAR OVERLOOKING THE GARDEN PROVIDES A PERFECT SETTING TO UNWIND WITH A DRINK. FOLLOWING PAGES: THE RECEPTION LOBBY HAS A GREEN MARBLE FLOOR INLAID WITH WHITE MARBLE; A BRASS CHANDELIER HANGS FROM THE CEILING OVER THE WATER FOUNTAIN; HAND-KNOTTED CARPET ADORNS THE FLOOR WHILE RELAXING ARMCHAIRS ARE DECORATED WITH SILK CUSHIONS.

230

BELOW: GUEST BEDROOMS HAVE GREEN MARBLE FLOORS; A COLONIAL CHEST OF DRAWERS IS PLACED ON THE OPPOSITE WALL WHILE THE ARMCHAIR SITS NEXT TO THE WINDOW OVERLOOKING THE GARDEN. **OPPOSITE PAGE, LEFT:** BELVEDERE IS A PRIVATE CLUB WHERE MEMBERSHIP IS BY INVITATION ONLY; ITS PLUSH SURROUNDINGS ARE CONDUCIVE TO MAJOR BUSINESS DEALS. **OPPOSITE PAGE, RIGHT:** ASIAN RESTAURANT.

The Kerala backwaters are a chain of brackish lagoons and lakes lying parallel to the Arabian Sea coast (known as the Malabar Coast) of Kerala state in southern India. The network includes five large lakes (including Ashtamudi Kayal and Vembanad Kayal) linked by 1500 km of canals, both man-made and natural, fed by 38 rivers, and extending virtually the entire length of Kerala. The backwaters were formed by the action of waves and shore currents, creating low barrier islands across the mouths of the many rivers flowing down the Western Ghats range. The port of Cochin (Cochin) is located at the lake's outlet to the Arabian Sea. Vembanad Lake is the largest of all the lakes, covering an area of 200 sq km, and bordered by Alappuzha (Alleppey), Kottayam, and Ernakulam districts. Vembanad Lake is designated a wetland of international importance under the Ramsar Convention.

'Vrinda' luxury boat sails in the picturesque waters of the lake and through the multitude palm-fringed canals that lead into it.

Connected by artificial canals, the backwaters form an economical means of transit, and a large local trade is carried on by inland navigation. Fishing, rice paddy and coir industries form an important economic backbone of this region. Traditional Kerala houseboats known as 'Kettuvallam'

239

('Kettu' means tied with ropes, and 'vallam' means boat in Malayalam) are the major tourist attraction in the backwaters. The boat is made of wooden planks joined and stitched together using coconut fibre ropes.

The outside of the boat is painted using cashew nut oil, which acts as a protective coating. During the time when road and rail transportation were expensive or unavailable, traders used this as a means of transportation in the inland waterways.

Alleppey town, sandwiched between the backwaters and the coast, is known as the 'Venice of the East' as it has a large network of canals that meander through it. The Vallam Kali (snake boat race) held every year in August is a major sporting attraction and is held during the harvest festival of Onam in the month of August.

Cochin is the most enchanting city of Kerala. Its natural harbour has attracted many voyagers since the Roman times. Its proximity to the tea, rubber, coffee and spices plantations has made it the commercial capital of Kerala. It used to be an important centre of the sea route between Europe and China. The Chinese influence is said to date back to the times of Kublai Khan when they introduced the unique Chinese fishing nets. The presence

240

of the Chinese must have been quite prominent, which is reflected in the vast quantities of Chinese pickle jars and antiques that are available. The culture of the city is very cosmopolitan, showing influences of Chinese, Jew, Arab, Portuguese, Dutch and English culture. This flavour is still evident in the Fort Cochin area, which houses an incredible number of Colonial buildings. Fortunately, it has been spared from the building frenzy, which can be seen in the Ernakulam region of the city.

The eventful history of this city began when a major cyclonic flood of 1341 opened the estuary at Cochin, till then a land-locked region, turning it into one of the finest natural harbours in the world. As a result, voyagers looked forward to visit this first truly international port of the Indian peninsula. Vasco da Gama, who discovered the sea route to India, lived in Fort Cochin. The Dutch ousted Portuguese in 1633 and finally the British took control of 'Princess of the Arabian Sea,' as the sailors lovingly called the city, from the Dutch in 1795.

Chinese fishing nets along the promenade in the Fort Cochin are the most photogenic landmarks of Cochin. The nets are erected on teak wood and bamboo poles and their working is controlled by huge stones tied to the

241

other end to provide a counter balance. These nets were brought here in the fourteenth century by the Chinese traders from the Court of Kublai Khan. During high tide, the area is buzzing with activity. Seafood shops sell their fresh catch, which you can buy and get cooked in one of the numerous stalls close by. Many of the old Colonial buildings in the Fort area have been lovingly restored, retaining the Colonial flavour, and opened as hotels. A few minutes' ride from Fort Cochin is the Mattencherry or the Jew Town. It is famous for its Dutch Palace, built by the Portuguese for the Hindu king in order to gain trading rights. Later, the Dutch restored it. It is an interesting museum with fabulous frescoes based on the Hindu epics painted on the walls. The highlight of this section is the Synagogue, the oldest in Asia. It has a colourful ambience with painted Chinese blue tiles on the floor and dozens of colourful chandeliers hanging from the ceiling. The Synagogue Street houses the few remaining families of Cochin Jews. It was once a dynamic community who excelled as the middlemen between the Europeans and the local population. The area is fast becoming a haven for antique dealers. Nearby, some old warehouses still deal with traditional spices. The strong aroma emanating from them will guide you to their door.

LUXURY CRUISER **THE OBEROI MOTOR VESSEL VRINDA** IS THE ONLY WAY TO EXPERIENCE THE BACKWATERS IN COMPLETE COMFORT. **PREVIOUS PAGES:** CHINESE FISHING NETS (CHEENA VALA) WERE BROUGHT BY THE CHINESE TRADERS TO COCHIN IN THE 15TH CENTURY; TILL TODAY, COCHIN IS THE ONLY PLACE OUTSIDE OF CHINA WHERE THIS FISHING APPARATUS IS USED; THE SETTING SUN PROVIDES A PERFECT FRAME TO SEE THESE UNIQUE FISHING NETS.

247

ABOVE: TEAK-PANELLED DECK IS A PERFECT PLACE TO WATCH THE DAILY LIFE OF THE FISHERMEN IN THE BACKWATERS AND CAPTURE THEM IN YOUR CAMERA. OPPOSITE PAGE: THE ROOMS ARE LUXURIOUS AND FILLED WITH MODERN COMFORTS LIKE AIR-CONDITIONING AND ATTACHED BATHROOMS; LARGE WINDOWS PROVIDE YOU WITH SWEEPING VIEWS OF THIS 'GOD'S OWN COUNTRY'. FOLLOWING PAGES: DAWN IS A PERFECT TIME TO EXPERIENCE THE GENTLE CALM THAT DESCENDS OVER THE PLACID WATERS OF THE VEMBANAD LAKE IN KERALA BACKWATERS. LUXURY CRUISER, 'THE OBEROI MOTOR VESSEL VRINDA' GLIDES GENTLY THROUGH THIS SCENIC BEAUTY.